Hello, My Name Is Mommy

Sheri Lynch

Hello,
My Name Is
Mommy

The Dysfunctional Girl's Guide to
Having, Loving *(and Hopefully Not
Screwing Up)* a Baby

St. Martin's Griffin 🦅 New York

www.stmartins.com

Book design by Michelle McMillian

ISBN 0-312-31832-4
EAN 978-0312-31832-1

First Edition: April 2004

10   9   8   7   6   5   4   3   2   1

For **Olivia** and **Caramia**
and Grandma Blackhair,
who left us too soon

Contents

Introduction

I learned two important things on my first visit to Rahway State Penitentiary. One, the doors really *do* clang shut behind you, just like in the movies, and two, it's not only the inmates who are treated like scum; their visiting families are, too. I went to Rahway to see my father, who was imprisoned for manufacturing crystal methamphetamine. His was a record bust for the time, and his mother, my grandma Blackhair, was devastated by his sentence. She held my hand as we made our way through the security checkpoints, jumping a little each time the metal doors slammed. The guards were unfriendly; they ignored her tentative smiles and greetings, and insisted on patting her down on the outside chance that she might have concealed a weapon in her dyed and teased updo.

We were briskly hustled into a cavernous, echoing cafeteria. Vending machines lined one wall, and row upon row of institutional tables filled the room. Every seat was taken. Young children careened through the crowd and scrambled on the floor. Babies, immobilized in plastic carriers, wailed or stared into the distance, pacifiers firmly planted in their tiny moon faces. The women talked, urgent, cajoling, as though a million unspoken words had built inside them only to erupt at this moment in this place. The din of their voices was unbearable. My father was waiting for us. His skin looked gray, and he was smaller than I remembered. He carefully smoked his Pall Malls and stared straight ahead, listening silently as his sister and mother chattered brightly about nothing, bits of neighborhood and family gossip.

Looking around with interest, I spotted a couple one table over heavily making out. The man was seated in a cheap plastic chair; the woman, who looked about nineteen, sat astride him, her long, floral-print skirt partially hiked up. With a start I realized that they were having sex while a toddler played with a handful of toy cars at their feet. My grandmother saw them too, and kicked me under the table. "Go get us a Coke or something," she said, rummaging in her purse for change. She eyed our fornicating neighbors and muttered, "It's a disgrace."

I made my way to the Coke machine. It was hard not to stare. Families were picnicking on the scarred tables; men cuddled and rocked infants. Some of the women were quietly crying. Some were obviously pregnant. One pudgy, sullen-faced young girl fed quarters into the snack machine with the practiced boredom of a retiree playing the Vegas slots. I watched with fascination as another girl, who looked about my age, gave a much older guy an enthusiastic blow job, the screen of her hair providing only minimal privacy. I was riveted: When you're nineteen and a nice Catholic school virgin, fellatio isn't something you see every day. My father caught me looking. "Cheryl!" he barked. "Get over here!" Embarrassed, I plunked the cold cans of soda onto the tabletop. "I don't want you coming here. I don't want you seeing this. Don't any of you come here, Jesus Christ." He furiously stubbed out his cigarette. "I mean, Jesus Christ, Ma. Goddamn it." The visit was over. I hugged him good-bye, his body stiff and unyielding as always. My father never liked to be hugged.

On the long drive home, my aunt silently smoked and maintained a speed just below the posted limit. Next to her in the front seat, my grandmother wept and blew her nose and invoked the Blessed Mother. I lay across the backseat, and stared out the window. The sky was the filthy, clotted gray of a New Jersey winter. The air in the car was foul with smoke. "Please stop crying, Gram," I pleaded. "It's not worth crying over, please." I was nineteen and in college and had all the answers. I pointed out that he'd done the crime, and that we were happier, less frightened now that he was out of the house. But she wasn't comforted. She sobbed and shook, and in a broken, raspy voice said, "He's my son. Someday you'll be a mother and you'll see. You'll see." With that, I pulled my jacket over my face and announced, "No, I won't. I am never having kids. Never."

September, 2000: I am crawling on my hands and knees in my room at the San Francisco Hilton. In less than an hour I'll take the elevator to the main ballroom downstairs where, though I don't know it yet, I'll lose the Marconi Award to Rush Limbaugh. Thrilling as it is to be nominated for the highest honor in the radio industry, right now all I care about is whether or not I can make it to the minibar without throwing up. Closing my eyes to stop the room from spinning, I drag myself queasily along the carpet. I have never been this ill—a tequila hangover pales in comparison. My whole body feels like one sickly-green, puffy bag full of churning and bubbling poison. Finally reaching the armoire, I rest my head against its cool wooden door and paw through the tiny refrigerator. Shuddering with revulsion at macadamia nuts and Bloody Mary mix, knocking M&M's and mini bottles aside,

I grab a can of Sprite and a small bag of pretzels. In the fetal position, my face resting on the floor, I slowly suck the salt off the pretzels and slurp weakly at the soda.

There was a time when I would have been horrified at the prospect of laying my cheek on a hotel room carpet. Now I welcome any germs that might be dwelling in the rug fibers, as long as they have the potential to kill me and put me out of this misery. I want to believe that this horror show of clammy nausea is the result of a bad shrimp or one too many glasses of red wine, but I know the truth. This is morning sickness. Trouble is, it's now almost 7:30 P.M., morning was a long time ago, and I've been sick around the clock for three days.

Somehow, I lurch to my feet and climb into a pair of croc-embossed leather pants. It's the last time they'll fit, but that's another thing I don't know yet, and anyway I'm too close to barfing to get sentimental over a pair of trousers. Tottering off to my date with defeat at the hands of Limbaugh, I think, if this is pregnancy I won't survive it. No one could be this sick for nine months and live.

I never liked baby dolls. Especially the kind with eyes that opened and closed. With their rigid plastic limbs and hard, unforgiving cheeks, they seemed like a ghastly parody of something human. I couldn't bear to have them watching me, and either hid them in the basement or turned their faces to the wall. Not that I spent much time playing at being a mommy. It didn't interest me. Dressing and undressing a doll, or wheeling it about in a carriage wasn't for me. If a game required that I have a baby, I simply dressed up a stuffed bear or dog, going so far as to clip up floppy ears in barrettes. The whole playing-house scene held no appeal. What was fun about pretending to do chores? One Christmas, Santa even brought me a play kitchen, complete with oven, refrigerator, and a working sink. There's a home movie out there somewhere that shows a five-year-old me scrubbing my toy dishes while sobbing my heart out. I hated it.

I was a career girl from the very start. Barbie dolls were my thing, and my Barbies led lives of real excitement, complete with offices and townhouses. My Barbies did important things like making other Barbies take dictation. They didn't marry Ken or settle down. They didn't dream of having babies of their own, and neither did I. Travel, adventure, a sports car, a career—these were my plans. It didn't hurt that my mom, a teen bride and a too-young mother of three, kept up a constant whisper in my ear about how I could do and be anything, that I didn't have to be a wife and mommy like her. I knew that there were so many things she never got to do, including college, because she'd gotten pregnant. In my childish mind, pregnancy somehow became mixed up with ruination, entrapment, and the end of dreams. Pregnant was what happened if you weren't careful. Kids were something that tied you down; a husband, an angry, weary creature that required enormous amounts of placating. *Don't make my mistakes* was the message, and though quietly and carefully delivered, I got it.

Life in our house wasn't exactly a glowing endorsement of parenthood. There was no disguising my mother's unhappiness, or my father's frustration. Both felt cheated by the hand they'd been dealt, and my two brothers and I were the unlucky cards. My father liked to tell me, "You were the only one we actually wanted. Your brothers were mistakes." Tough news for them, slim comfort for me, and not much of a fairy tale for any of us. We suspected early on that we were a pain in the ass, an expense, and a trap that had forever ensnared our parents. We learned to keep our heads down and stay clear of their increasing hostilities. The marriage lasted seventeen years, ending in a firestorm of tears, gunfire, infidelity, threats, pleas, and curses. I was twelve when my father met me at the school bus, gave me fifteen minutes to pack, and took me away. It would be sixteen years before I saw my mother again. In those sixteen years I watched my father spiral down into the cocaine and methamphetamine addictions that ultimately put him behind bars. I survived his coke jags, his crazed threats, his rages, even his holding my grandmother and me at gunpoint for hours. I survived DEA raids, a stint on welfare, and enough fear and melodrama to last a lifetime. I finished high school, waited tables to pay for college, grew up, and got out.

Then I got pregnant. That it happened in my midthirties when I was married—and happily—for the second time didn't make it any less terrifying. Only now my fear wasn't that pregnancy would ruin my life, but that I, in my ignorance and with a lifetime's dysfunction behind me, would ruin the life of an innocent unborn baby. What did I know about babies? What did I know about pregnancy? Nothing. As I always have, I turned to books. There is no shortage of tomes on childbirth. From careful, scientific explanations of chromosomes and stretch marks to airy, sentimental odes on the serene fecundity of females, pregnancy and birth have been thoroughly covered. Or have they? I read every book printed and not one told me what it would really feel like. Not one told me what a screwed-up working girl like me could truly expect. Other mothers weren't much help. They answered my questions with vague non-answers like "I don't really remember" or "Everybody's different" or "That was a long time ago" or "It's a love like no other," or my personal favorite, "You'll just know what to do when the time comes."

All of the books promised that having a child would forever change me—they just didn't explain how. After a lifetime spent relying on the printed word to make sense of my world, I came up empty. As the months slipped away and I grew ever more rotund, I made a vow. I would write this pregnancy-birth-mommy experience down as I went.

I'd try to remember every bit of it so that when some other misfit mom-to-be asked me what it was really like, I'd be able to tell her. Because when you're afraid of doing to your baby what was done to you, when you lie awake at night worrying that you're incapable of the unselfish love and nurturing that the child growing inside you requires, then a clear understanding of cell division and the role of the placenta is no comfort at all. What you need, in those sleepless, pregnant hours is the warm knowledge that someone even nuttier and less competent than you has done it—and survived. Thrived, even.

I embarked on my mommy adventure as a newly pregnant professional woman with a killer wardrobe. I was rapidly transformed into a fearful and fearsome waddling beast. Nine months later (actually, ten—the whole nine-month concept is a lie), I was an awestruck and overcome new mother, trying to write everything down, not wanting to lose anything to the fog of fatigue and emotion that results in a kind of maternal amnesia. I posted my writings on my radio program Web site, and an amazing thing happened. Women from all over the country began writing to me, sharing their own stories, and telling me how my columns had made them laugh, cry, and remember. Strangers stopped me at the grocery store to tell me that until they'd read what I'd written about my C-section, they'd had no words to describe their own. I'd find myself hugging women I'd known only a few minutes, the two of us blinking back tears. Over and over again women told me, "I thought I was the only one who felt this way." Somebody ought to write a book, I'd respond.

So I did. *Hello, My Name Is Mommy* is for every woman who has struggled through pregnancy, childbirth, and motherhood feeling like a big, clumsy, incompetent fraud. It's for women who had no idea what an infant really was, much less what to do with one. It's for women who never imagined themselves as mommies, and for mommies who've forgotten just how inept they once were. It's for women who were raised on raw hot dogs, Cheerios, secondhand cigarette smoke, and the desperate unhappiness of their own mothers. It's for women like me who never dreamed how much joy and fulfillment might come with the role of mommy—a role we'd spent our adult lives fearing, even resisting.

On my bumpy and neurotic journey to motherhood, I discovered something amazing about pregnancy, something carefully hidden beneath all the layers of pastel sentiment and cutesy bunnies-and-duckies rhetoric of the maternity marketplace: power. There is no creature on earth more powerful, more imbued with raw, primal humanity than the woman who carries, births, and nurses an infant. No one. A mother is a roaring engine of life, a maker and symbol of messy, bloody, wrenching miracles. Yet we hide her behind the kind of infantile whimsy that marks so much of the pregnancy experience. At her most potent, we insist that she become sexless, and worse, childlike. On top of that, working women are made to feel apologetic for having obeyed the clumsy and unproductive dictates of our biology. Mommies are relegated to the sidelines as creatures who are no longer clever, interesting, or sexy. That's worse than unfair; it's a complete fraud.

The nursery is our foxhole, motherhood our battlefield. Every woman who becomes a mommy is a warrior, forever transformed. While we celebrate the exploits of soldiers, we roll our eyes and dismiss women who share their birth and parenting stories with a scornful "All they do is talk about babies." Having a child opened my eyes. How could the most elemental of human experiences be reduced to an opportunity for shopping and decorating? How, after creating a life inside our bodies and nourishing it at our breasts, are we supposed to *not* talk about that? How can we be expected to remain unchanged?

And how, once we return to work, are we to respond to inane comments like, "I guess you'll be all focused on the baby now, right?"

Whether our children are of our bodies or of our hearts, what matters is that we're mommies—and we're good at it. Even the most dysfunctional Misfits are capable of loving and nurturing a child. We're strong, brave, sexy—goddesses, if you want to know the truth. All of the rotten, insane, slipshod nonsense we endured as children gave us more than just fodder for counseling. It gave us insight, wisdom, and humor. It made us resourceful. Although we didn't realize it at the time, it helped transform us into warriors. Now we're mommies—and we're taking our power back.

1

A Good Poke in the Eye

It was a bottomless sleep, the kind of drooling, narcotized slumber known only to shift workers, summering teenagers, and the mothers of small babies. This was a thick, pillow-faced oblivion that claimed me, not so much restful as desperate. I might have remained unconscious in the same position for hours longer, maybe even days, had it not been for the moist thumb that was gingerly peeling back my eyelid. Instinctively I jerked my head away, still lost in a fog of dreamless exhaustion. But the thumb came again, this time poking into my eye as it pulled the lid up. A giant, blurry cartoon of a face swam into view, all fuzzy halo and cheeks, toothless, with enormous blue eyes. I shrank away, but the thumb was relentless, yanking my eyelid up toward my hairline. Panicking, and with both eyes open now, I struggled to fit together who and where I was. Was I being probed? Tortured? Drugged? Was there any hope of escape? Then my blurry tormentor leaned in closer and I could smell its sweet, faintly milky breath. "Mama!" it crowed, face splitting into a wide, gummy grin. "Mama! Mama! Mama!" Relief flooded my body. This was no alien seeking to harvest my eyeballs, but only my eight-month-old daughter deciding that it was time for mommy to wake up and join the fun. I pulled her onto my chest for a hug and tickled her under her plump chin. She squealed and giggled and patted my face with her damp little hands. If you can live with the occasional sharp poke in the eye, babies make the perfect alarm clocks—no snooze button, no batteries to wear out, and no denying when sleepy time is over. Good morning, mommy!

It took no time at all for my wild baby girl to teach me that every expectation I had regarding parenthood was off base. Instead of allowing herself to be propped up in various charming poses—the better to model her many chic ensembles—she made it clear that she hadn't come into this world merely to be decorative, but to spend every waking moment in my arms. Rather than snoozing the days away while her daddy and I carefully researched the optimal intellect-building toys (or slept, ate, and showered), she insisted on remaining happily alert, her eyes never leaving our faces. She stood on our laps from birth, her legs wobbly but strong, so determined to finish anything she started. She scared us a little, to be truthful, especially me.

My first mistake came in assuming that newborns arrived without much personality to speak of, that it took them a bit to turn into people. I thought she might loll about in a knit jumper like a sweetly scented blob while I caught my breath and tried to figure the whole scene out. Wrong. Right from the start I fumbled everything, from the sticky tabs on her diapers (baby lotion renders them instantly useless), to the bewildering array of snaps on her pajamas (imagine cramming an octopus into a bagpipe). When I scratched her leg with the sharp prong of my engagement ring, the sight of her little face twisting in pain nearly ripped the heart from my chest. Afraid of burning her, I made her bath water too cold. Afraid of starving her, I woke her repeatedly to eat. Afraid of dropping her, I squeezed her too tightly.

Holding her in my arms, I couldn't believe that she was really mine, and I wanted to gobble her up, from her wee niblet toes to the silky and fragrant crown of her head. She made me deliriously happy—and horribly afraid. This was more than an awesome responsibility; this was an actual life, gazing at me with complete trust, deeply interested in whatever I planned to do next. Knowing me, how could I not botch it up?

I wanted more than anything to be a good mother, but I knew that good intentions alone wouldn't get the job done. Not with my background, riddled with the kinds of dysfunction more common to gangsta rap and good old-fashioned country music than any middle-class family fairy tale you're likely to hear. My mental home movies are filled with action-packed scenes of lying and leaving, guns and police, drugs and coked-out, barely legal girls with semen smeared on their faces—a picture made complete with the requisite seamy visits to daddy in prison. It was enough to convince me that I might make a poor candidate for parenthood—even pet ownership seemed like a dicey proposition.

Face it: You know when you're screwed up, when you've got issues, baggage, unresolved conflicts. You know when you're damaged goods, even if no one else can tell—*particularly* if no one else can tell. Having spent my twenties as a ticking time bomb of maternal neurosis waiting to happen, I slid into therapy and my thirties panic-stricken at the thought of having—and possibly hurting—a family. And I was tired enough for someone twice my age. Tired of running in place, of making everything seem perfect when it was anything but. I'd been screaming, "I can do it!" my whole life, but I washed up on a therapist's doorstep whimpering just the opposite. I felt like one of the poorly made or damaged toys in the old stop-motion animation Christmas special *Rudolph the Red-Nosed Reindeer*, the ones who banished themselves to a lonely island, a haven for a Charlie-in-the-box (as opposed to "Jack") or a train with square wheels. I was a misfit toy too, and it was time to admit it.

We're the girls who've ducked the toughest punches thrown our way, the lost girls who've beaten the odds, the products of broken homes and ruined families. We're the ones they counted out. Except, we were different. Somehow we turned the booze, drugs, violence, deceit, abandonment, abuse, or apathy of our early lives into the foundation for something strong and resilient, something good. We transformed ourselves from victims into survivors. Now, all grown up, we look perfectly normal, better than normal even. Competent. Driven. Focused. Disciplined. Perfectionist, high-achieving go-getters. Bred in chaos, we're now the rock in a crisis. Too bad we don't feel that way on the inside. That dark place is a jumble of noise and emotion, a place where we are terrified of repeating history.

What do we know about nurturing, stability, or patience? Our deepest fear is that we're too ruined to be good mothers, a fear that's magnified every time we open a magazine or flick on the television only to find yet another expert explaining how abused kids tend to grow up to be abusers themselves. It doesn't matter that friends and colleagues consider us the undisputed master of the three C's: calm, competent, and confident. The voices in our heads are screaming something else, and it's that message of fear and craven lunacy that you really believe. *Screwed up*, it says. *Ugly, stupid, useless, selfish. Not good enough, phony, fake, a fraud.* Success, cash, toys—nothing drowns out that voice for long. Motherhood, the biggest, most awesome and overwhelming challenge in life might only make it louder, at least temporarily.

Even those lucky enough to have grown up in ideal Beaver Cleaver–type families have their own lurid tales to tell. There are plenty of Misfit Moms who never laid eyes on a pistol or a parole officer yet still feel like imposters, ill-equipped for parenthood, for responsibilities that seem to come so naturally to others. A Misfit friend from a happily intact family with no woeful stories in her past said of herself, "I'm like an incompetent nervous freak in a human costume. What could I ever do with a baby but screw it up?" Misfits may be born or made, but one thing's for sure: although the Misfit Mom-to-be may look like every other hip chick browsing in Baby Gap, inside, we know we're different. Churning, giddy to be pregnant, despairing of our own inadequacies, scared, worried, and overjoyed all at once. This is the emotional whiplash of the Misfit Mom-to-be. It would be wonderful to enjoy a serene and Buddhalike gestation, but who are we kidding? The Misfit path is never that smooth. It's always twisted, rocky, and strictly uphill. But this time, you really don't have to climb alone.

Looking back, let's be honest and acknowledge that our parents didn't give having kids much serious thought. They didn't have strategies or philosophies. What they had was little or no effective contraception, which is how most of us made it into the world. Children today are widely viewed as precious bundles of raw potential, treasures, the very hope and soul of the future. We, on the other hand, were mouths to feed—mouths that at any moment might dare to speak, possibly bringing shame and embarrassment or worse upon the whole family. That's not to say that our parents didn't love us. They did, in their own way, though it's tough to argue that their love wasn't always of the unconditional variety. In fact, a good many of us were made to take better care of them than they ever took of us.

Lacking the sane, predictable security that kids require in order to grow up healthy and whole, we cobbled together another sort of life, one built on lies. There were the lies we told neighbors, teachers, and the parents of our friends, and the worst lies of all, the ones we told ourselves. We lived a double life, split on one side by screaming or violence or terror, and on the other by excuses, pleas, and promises not kept. We teetered in the middle, learning to control what little we could, keeping our hair and clothes clean, finishing our schoolwork on time. Too many of us became the products of the broken homes, the first children of divorce—the weary and scarred progeny of a generation's worth of scarily unfit parents.

Our families split up when divorce was new, before anyone had had a chance to figure out the rules. We paid the price, not just in shame and self-doubt, but also in the dreary wagonloads of baggage that we've been hauling behind us ever since. We can't help but wonder: Will I be the same as my mother or father? Is there some psychological or genetic trigger buried deep within me that will one day go off, turning me into the kind of parent who hits, or screams, or hurts, or just plain leaves? Is it possible to be wired for that, to be doomed by one's own history? To answer *yes* is to give up, to admit defeat, something no Misfit worthy of the name has ever done. Overcoming the past may not lie just in making peace with it, but in rethinking it altogether. Can we cast ourselves as heroes instead of victims? Can we turn an inventory of dysfunction into one of strength? I think we can, and the sooner you believe it, the sooner you can harness your considerable Misfit power for good—your own good.

The trouble with Misfits is that we sometimes lack clarity on what is acceptable versus unacceptable behavior. Having grown up under battle conditions, we tend to confuse the criminal with the quirky, or view as typical what any sane person would consider appalling. For example, your dad wearing a lampshade on his head after a few too many slugs of scotch is quirky. Your dad reaching for a loaded pistol and shooting the lampshade full of smoking holes is criminal. See the difference? If you grew up in the latter family, it may be a challenge to separate the two. Misfits are so used to making excuses and lies to cover the trashy or terrifying truth that we can lose sight of just how ghastly our origins were. Since there are so many varieties of dysfunctional Misfit experience (and I've been fortunate enough to experience many firsthand, with the possible exceptions of alcoholism, bestiality, and devil worship—and I still wonder if I didn't get a little taste of that last one), it might be helpful to review the following examples of typical, utterly appalling, and criminal behavior.

Target shooting: *typical. Quirky, but typical.*

Target shooting using your child's dolls or toys as targets: *Utterly appalling.*

Target shooting in the house using your spouse as the target: *Criminal.*

Parents shrieking, howling, and screaming at each other: *Typical.*

Parents cursing, denouncing, and openly threatening each other: *Utterly appalling.*

Parents cursing, denouncing, and openly threatening their kids: *Criminal.*

A beer after work, a glass or two of wine with dinner: *Typical.*

Three bottles of wine, dinner forgotten, kids left to fend for themselves: *Utterly appalling.*

A bottle of Jack, mommy passed out on the couch in her own puke: *Criminal.*

A parent lights a cigarette while taking care of baby: *Typical.*

A parent lights a water bong while baby sobs in playpen: *Utterly appalling.*

A parent lights the couch on fire in rage over partner's infidelity: *Criminal.*

Emotional, verbal, physical, and substance abuse are the arsenal of weapons in any unholy family war. Shell-shocked veterans, Misfits have seen it all: the broken glass, the empty bottles, the yelling, slamming, drinking and drugging; the social workers and sheriff's deputies; and for a lucky few, the spectacle of a parent tricked out in an orange county-jail jumpsuit being paraded on the local television news. Is it so surprising that we're afraid to have children of our own? We don't know what normal looks or feels like. We don't know how good mommies and daddies behave. Healthy, functioning families are things we've only seen on television, or glimpsed with longing through the windows of other people's homes. Our own houses were never so tranquil. The Misfit Mom-to-be understands all too well how swiftly a home can turn into a frightening place, and how easily children become the casualties of raging adult battles. We know the sorrow, powerlessness, and fatigue that come from having no means of escape. What we don't always know is how strong all of that has made us. Having godawful parents does not guarantee that you'll be one, too. It just means you'll have to work a little harder to master all the basics you missed the first time around.

Misfits not only tell the best stories, they make the greatest friends, because there's nothing you can do or say to shock them. This also happens to be an extremely useful characteristic in a mommy. My dearest friend Marsha survived two helplessly alcoholic parents, put herself through college on a full scholarship, is raising a pair of bright and beautiful children, and is the one person to have on hand should anything catch on fire, or require bail money, stitches, or mouth-to-mouth resuscitation. After a childhood spent prying empty bottles out of her unconscious mother's hands, and mopping up enough regurgitated Kentucky bourbon to fill a wading pool, Marsha is a mommy who can handle anything a baby might spew.

Inspirational Misfit stories are everywhere. I met a gorgeous older woman in a grocery store whose father used to practice his amateur knife-throwing act in their kitchen, using beer as a lubricant and her mother as a target. Today, she's polished, successful—and the mother of smart, healthy, high-achieving children. My own father once held me, my grandmother, and my boyfriend's asthmatic and obese Chihuahua, Buckwheat, at gunpoint in the kitchen for over two hours. He was in full-blown freebase psychosis, raving and cursing, threatening to kill us all—starting with "that goddamn wheezing dog." Poor Buckwheat. I turned out okay, if having a college degree, an amazing career, an adoring husband, and delightful and healthy kids fits the definition.

My sister-in-law found herself homeless at fifteen after an ugly divorce distracted her parents to the point of forgetting she existed. Today she's a happily married mother of five whose oldest son is pursuing a graduate degree at an Ivy League school. Not bad for the little girl who had nowhere to sleep or eat, and no one who gave a damn either way. Would it shock you to discover that a top executive at an internationally renowned company somehow blossomed despite years of physical and emotional abuse at the hands of her genuinely psychotic mother? Or that the nice lady who cuts your hair, and has photos everywhere of her twin baby boys, spent her adolescence taking care of three younger siblings because her father was gone and her mother was too wasted on crack to care for the kids? In ten years of doing the *Bob & Sheri* show on radio, I've heard countless similar stories, some worse, some scarier, but all told by clever, resourceful women with this in common: They are survivors. Perhaps the best that can be said about our miserably colorful childhoods is that they were pure exercises in building character. Lucky us, with so much character and street smarts to spare. Lucky us, knowing what it truly means to go too far.

Misfit Moms look back on the wreckage of our early lives with a mixture of grief and pride. Grief for all that was wasted or squandered, for all the times our youthful and trusting hearts were dropped and broken. Pride, for the stunning and often miraculous ways in which we overcame our trashy and tragic odds. Misfits are tough and intuitive, able to spot each other using a sort of sixth sense. I met my friend Anne that way. Anne is the ultimate Misfit Mom, so freaked out by the ever-present specter of tragedy that her daughter wasn't allowed to eat grapes, hot dogs, olives, or hard candy until she was four years old—that's how convinced Anne was that her baby was destined to choke to death. We worked together in different departments at a television station, and circled each other like wary bears until one day agreeing to hook up after hours for a drink. We weren't halfway into a bottle of wine before the revelations were flowing. "I'll see you your junkie father and missing mother," Anne offered, "and raise you my alcoholic father—also out of the picture—my overprotective mother who wouldn't even let us have a color television for fear that it might explode and blind us, and," here she paused for effect, "my aunt, the nun!" To claim a relative who is an actual living, breathing nun represents a level of repression that's hard to beat. She had me.

With our demented stories, and a view of the world that tends to the dark and twisted, Misfits need to find and support each other. There's nothing more depressing than baring your soul to a so-called normal woman, only to see her become completely bug-eyed and uncomfortable. Misfits need a friend who understands where we've been, and how nervous we are about where we might yet go. The pregnant Misfit needs this most of all, being essentially a jumpy bundle of hormones, worries, fears, and irrational broodings. Without a sense of humor and some trusted support, she's likely to be a basket case. Having walked and waddled down that path, I know how bumpy and scary it can be. I'm not a shrink, and can't offer happy meds or an

You Turned Out Just Fine

All parents make mistakes, and that's a good thing. If they didn't, none of us would have any funny stories to tell at parties. You'll make lots of mistakes, too. There is a critical difference, though, between you and your parents. You will analyze your mistakes to death and ultimately blame yourself for everything from your toddler's bed-wetting, to your teenager's pierced tongue, to your adult child's inability to find and keep a job. Your parents, on the other hand, are wonderfully free of such psychological torment. They consider the having—and subsequently not killing—of children as proof enough of a job well done. No matter what kind of loony monkeyshines they perpetrated on you and your siblings, your parents will always take cover behind their five favorite words: You Turned Out Just Fine. Was their idea of dentistry a whiskey-soaked wad of cotton and some late-night TV watching? Not to worry: YTOJF. Root beer in your baby bottle? YTOJF. Home alone for hours on end with an unlocked gun cabinet? You kids damn well knew better than to get into Daddy's prized hunting rifles! Oh, and by the way? You Turned Out Just Fine. Whether it was creepy Uncle Frank getting a little too friendly after a couple of beers, the sheriff banging on the door while you readied the latest lie, or taking a drag off of your mom's Marlboro because really, is there anything more hilarious than watching a six-year-old attempt to smoke? You survived it all. As your parents love to point out, You Turned Out Just Fine. And we did. Okay, so we're a little twitchy and high-strung and prone to poor judgment in matters of love. But at least we know better than to go looking for sympathy from our parents. They'll only fall back on their *second* favorite line of defense: You Always Were a Drama Queen.

exact map out of your personal wilderness. But I can walk with you, point out some good scenery along the way, and share a few tips that might make your journey a little easier.

One thing I can promise is to never use fruit analogies to describe the size or shape of your uterus, and trust me, I'm incapable of finding the poetry in your ripe, fecund, rapidly expanding form. There are plenty of pregnancy books out there for that. This Misfit Mom looked like a walrus, felt like a breed sow, chugged orange juice straight out of the carton, and shuffled around the house bellowing demands at her increasingly alarmed husband. If my pregnancy were a poem, it could only have consisted of words rhyming with *barf*, *bloat*, and *beast*.

How do you transform your Misfit baggage into your secret mommy weapon? Begin by refusing to apologize for who you are or where you come from. Call things by their proper names, even when those names are ugly and awful. *Especially* when they're ugly and awful. Fear and self-doubt are gluttons for deceit; starve them to the bone. Whatever hellhole you were spawned and raised in is no longer your shameful secret to keep. That was your boot camp, your own private slice of Darwinism—and look who was strong enough to survive! The very same skills that pulled you through a rough childhood, that enabled you to push forward when a weaker, less determined girl would have fallen back, are the ones that you'll call on now to be a good mommy.

The beauty of the Misfit way is that the worst that can happen to you probably already has. That means that it's time for new labels. Instead of *damaged* or *crippled*, think *seasoned* and *ready*. Trade dewy illusions about the instant fulfillment an infant can bring for a realist's understanding of the hard challenges and rich rewards that can be ours when we commit to loving and living fully. Know that, regardless of your past, you deserve the love of family, and the comforts of a peaceful home. It's never too late or too hard to open your hands and seize what has been waiting for you all along. There is no sweeter balm for the battered Misfit heart than the love you will feel for your own child. There you'll find redemption and healing that no lover, no paycheck, and no prescription can ever equal.

The Incredible Egg

Unlike sperm, which are produced almost continuously throughout a male's lifetime, we are born with every single egg we will ever have. A pessimist would note that our eggs are therefore every bit as old as we are and that there's no time to waste in having a baby. But there's another, more magical way to look at it. Your body contains multitudes, to paraphrase the poet Walt Whitman. The child that you conceive is no stranger new to the world, but someone who has been with you always. Your little egg has shared your journey, and by the miracles of timing and fertilization, will now share your life.

If that egg happens to become a daughter, you will add a link to an amazing genetic chain. There is a specific kind of DNA called *mitochondrial DNA* that passes unchanged from mother to daughter. You have your mother's mitochondrial DNA, and her mother's, and her mother's and so on all the way back to your original female ancestor. Your daughter will have it too, as will her daughters as far into the future as your progeny are able to reproduce. It's a bit like looking into an endlessly repeating funhouse mirror. It's also a form of immortality. And it's something unique to women. Think about that next Mother's Day.

When you consider how many awe-inspiring and miraculous events occur inside the female body, the irritations we're forced to endure—like cramps, bloating, bleeding, cellulite, pantyhose—seem pretty minor. Our bodies are the cauldrons and cradles of life. All in all, it's great to be a girl.

Whether it's a thumb in my eye, or the wettest, most drooling kiss on my cheek, every minute spent with my daughter has been a gift of pure joy. She is my tiny egg, my perfect wish made real, and the best, most glorious time I've ever had. Even when she's throwing up on me, or wiping her runny nose on my sleeve, or stroking my clean hair with a yogurt-dipped hand. Babies are like that. You'll be surprised at just how much fun they can be. Now let's get busy and go have one.

2
Where Babies Come From

If my family had spent generations hoarding gold the way they hoarded inhibition and shame I'd never have to work a day in my life. Instead, we were poor in dollars but rich in repression. It's a bad combination. The obvious culprit in our uptight saga is the Catholic Church. We were all well schooled in the concepts of chastity, decency, virtue, and virginity. But even the Pope can't shoulder the blame for the weird cocktail of nuttiness that we concocted from it. In our family, sex was the big, nasty, evil cause of every possible flavor of ruination. Sex led to pregnancy, which led to marriage, which led to misery. Sex laid such a cunning trap for a woman that she could scarcely avoid whorishness. Sex was everything and nothing, was hinted at and whispered of, and never openly acknowledged. Sex was dirty and bad. Unless it wasn't, which was seldom and very tricky to calculate since even sex in the context of marriage had its filthy aspects. The most innocent displays of physical affection were viewed with suspicion and distaste, particularly if they occurred between a father and his pubescent daughter.

No one seems to know how our clan got so twisted, since speaking openly about the past was considered an act of treachery. Once, in an effort to understand why we were so weird, I asked Grandma Blackhair if there was some horrible family secret involving incest or cousins getting married—anything that might explain our collective craziness. She shuddered, made the sign of the cross over her lips, and waved me away with a stern warning to "mind your business, Miss College Lips." In this murky environment of secrecy and superstition, the shocking revelation of my mother's adultery was considered proof of the wicked weakness of women. The aunts and cousins shook their heads in sorrow and disbelief, while privately whispering, in the crazy-making doublespeak of our family, "My God, who could blame her?" Fear, loathing, confusion, ignorance—could there be a less ideal setting for an education in matters sexual? That education consisted of the following nuggets of wisdom:

1. According to my tenth-grade health teacher, a boy suffering from a state of arousal was an irrational, unpredictable beast. The teenage boy with an erection was best dealt with in the same manner one would employ to handle a rabid raccoon: Avoid eye contact, make no sudden movements, and back slowly away before alerting the authorities.

2. According to my beloved Grandma Blackhair, a boy wanted only One Thing and would say or do anything to achieve his lusty ends, including, but not limited to, begging a girl to let him "just park it there for a minute," an arrangement that would surely lead to pregnancy even though no intercourse had occurred. Grandma Blackhair gave me a beautiful garnet ring for my sixteenth birthday, the specific purpose of which was to forcefully jab the engorged member of any boy who

tried to get too frisky. Of course, the defense of my virtue was solely my burden to bear, since again, the aroused teenage boy was basically an animal.

3. According to my father, every girl had a tickle or an itch (his vulgar characterization of the female sex drive) and was an easy target for the aroused teenage boy, who was, you guessed it, a worthless sex-mad primate stopping at nothing to achieve his pleasure. Of course, if I wanted to be a whore like my mother, that was my choice since the apple really didn't fall far from the tree, did it?

It's easy to understand why I might have been a little shy in the bedroom. But years of reading *Cosmopolitan* magazine taught me that there had to be a wild nymphomaniac living somewhere inside me if only I could reach her. Unfortunately, she was buried beneath tons of Nice Girls Don't, If I Do That He'll Think I'm a Tramp, and Only Sluts Ask For It. Digging her out took more strength than I possessed. Even if I was sometimes able to lure her into the light with tequila, lingerie, or handcuffs, she only came to play, never to stay. Therapy helped, but only to a point, since even the most devoted therapist won't pop into your bedroom and tell your husband what you want sexually— assuming you even know. And if he or she offers to, it's unethical and a threesome, which is exactly the kind of promiscuous and destructive behavior that pushed you into therapy to begin with.

When it comes to inhibition, the repressed girl is on her own in finding a cure. Luckily, there are lots of good strategies to try. Since I was too uncoordinated for pole dancing, and not energetic enough for a job at Nevada's Bunny Ranch, I opted for a second marriage to a nice mechanical engineer from the Midwest who, poor thing, had no idea what he was getting into. Inside the protective cocoon of a good marriage, one based on mutual respect and honesty, I loosened up a lot. I even took to wearing skimpy little things trimmed in fur, and dared the occasional outright come-on in assorted public places. He liked my early attempts at nympho abandon quite a bit, even if he didn't understand the point of doing it in the woods when we had a perfectly nice bed waiting at home. (Ah, the famed midwestern practicality!) And he was puzzled by the scrupulous care I took in the course of a day to avoid brushing against or otherwise touching his genital area. I tried to explain how even accidentally touching "it" would leave him aroused and in a state of mindless erotic savagery, which seemed a cruel and potentially dangerous thing to do if I wasn't able or willing to follow through. He reacted with mild incredulity—okay, not really. He thought my theory was insane. Whacked. Twisted and bizarre. And it is. See how hard some lessons are to unlearn?

Having never had unprotected sex, not once in my entire life, I was curious to see if it felt any different. Would it be wilder? Freer? More organic? Maybe it was my subconscious fear of pregnancy that had been holding me back all along! Maybe I'd been so distracted by the need to prevent pregnancy that I'd missed the best part of sex. It was supposed to be fun and easy, not serious or stressful. That it was mixed up in my head with eternal damnation was not the fault of sex, any more than sex could be blamed for the lurid warnings Grandma Blackhair frequently issued, all of which began with the phrase, "Your grandfather learned some very filthy tricks while he was in the Navy." Not only would trying for a baby represent legal sex, sex for the very reason the whole act was invented, but it would also feel like gambling: a little dangerous, a little chancy, and very exciting. I couldn't wait to throw my pills away and discover the real me, a wild, grownup woman unhampered by silly superstitions or outdated ideas of proper behavior.

Imagine my disappointment at discovering that the Pill-less me was exactly the same awkward and uptight creature as before. Not only did procreative fornication fail to automatically deliver me to the heights of passion common in romance novels, it actually gave me an entirely new reason to feel inadequate. Somewhere along the way, I'd gotten the idea that I would know the very instant that conception occurred. I blame this wacky notion on all the earthy, crunchy women I've met and read about who claim to have felt the very spark of life ignite inside their wombs. I desperately wanted to be one of them. This fantasy relied heavily on my much vaunted, but seldom seen, female intuition, not to mention an almost uncanny sensitivity to the workings of my own body. It was supposed to go like this: After a fabulous lovemaking session in which I was rendered insensate (after being ravished and tumbling off the cliffs of ecstasy and so on), I would feel the fruitful collision of sperm and egg, touch my abdomen in wonder and whisper, "Darling, we're going to have a baby!" Then we'd celebrate our joyful news with a little wheatgrass juice and some aromatherapy candles.

None of this happened. Being the sort of woman who routinely discovers scrapes and bruises on her body with no clear idea of how they got there, I must have been high to think that I'd know the moment a microscopic sperm and egg made contact in a part of my body I probably couldn't locate on a guess. Another disappointing discovery: Sex without the Pill is just like sex with the Pill, only more purposeful and enthusiastic. Meaning, you're more enthusiastic about it. Frequency and timing take center stage at baby-making time, leaving pleasure and inventiveness a distant second and third. This is normal, and by all accounts it only gets worse the longer it takes for a couple to conceive. One woman I know put her husband on a beeper so that he could be summoned instantly should she find herself in a state of maximum fer-

Smells Like Teen Spirit

Groundbreaking new research shows that sperm possess receptors that draw them to chemical signals given off by eggs, leading, of course, to conception. Interestingly, sperm may also be attracted to certain specific scents, including lily of the valley. No word on how we're to spritz our microscopic eggs with *eau de* lily, but the implications are staggering. The discovery that natural chemical attractants may play a part in the mating dance of sperm and egg sparks hope for new breakthroughs in the field of assisted reproduction. A listener scoffed at this bit of science, noting, "So, based on my two ex-husbands, my eggs must be attracted to Drakkar Noir? That's great—even my eggs have lousy taste."

tility. This man referred to himself as "Sperm-on-the-Hoof" and wasn't nearly as delighted to be paged for sex as you might think. He complained of not getting enough foreplay. He whined about having to help her stand on her head afterward. He worried that sex would never be fun and easy again. He agonized about the yearning on his wife's face whenever they spotted a toddler at the grocery store or a restaurant. When you long for a baby of your own, every day that you don't get pregnant is a disappointment. Talk about pressure!

Add to that the recent revelation that the medical profession was, um, wrong about the whole women and fertility thing. All that stuff about it being okay to delay childbearing until the midthirties and beyond? A mistake. Sorry. It turns out that women are dramatically less fertile after age thirty-five. Those women in their mid-to-late forties that we keep reading about who are having beautiful, healthy babies with ease? Now they tell us the majority of those women have had to rely on donor eggs. Now they tell us that we should have had our babies when we were young and fertile. We're even beginning to hear whispered suggestions that women delay starting their careers until after they've conceived their children. Ouch. Kind of a different message than the one *we* got. We were so determined not to fall into the same trap that ensnared our mothers that we fell into another, completely new one: we ran out of time. I used to wear a t-shirt with a comic book–style illustration of a beautiful blonde clutching her head and exclaiming, "I forgot to have kids!" I thought it was hip and ironic. I didn't know it was prophetic.

Infertility is heartbreaking, but not always hopeless. Amazing things are being done in the field of assisted reproduction, and every day children are born to couples that, even ten years ago, would have had no hope of conceiving. I talked to a specialist in the field who shared the following advice: If you are anywhere in your thirties and have been trying without success for six months to have a baby, seek help. Every day is precious when it comes to your fertility. Nature may take its course, but it may also need a little assistance. Don't wait years, as some hopeful couples do. And don't give up your dreams of motherhood if your body refuses to cooperate. There are too many babies around the world in need of loving parents. Adoption is a gift for everyone involved. I know what I'm talking about: My husband was adopted, and no mommy was ever more joyous or fulfilled than his on the morning he was placed in her arms. There are some deluded souls who think that being a mommy is all about biology. Misfits had to learn the hard way that when it comes to children, biology isn't worth a damn without daily, faithful, committed love. Being pregnant is a very small part of a mommy's job, and as important and wonderful as pregnancy is, it's not the whole story. It's barely the prequel. Love isn't a product of your uterus, but of your heart and mind. Only a fool would allow the limits of her body to dictate the limits of her heart.

End of lecture, since it's a little insane to get science, medical, or family planning information from someone like me. Instead, I'll share what I did to speed things along.

I went off the Pill on my honeymoon. I know—so old-fashioned and quaint, but fitting for the first non-pregnant bride in the history of my family. My new husband and I snorkeled, swam, drank silly rum drinks decorated with paper umbrellas, and took long walks in the island moonlight. Intoxicated by our tropical surroundings (if a bit disappointed not to have been magically transformed into a nympho-

Stretching Your Odds . . .

When you're trying to conceive, you're likely to get a whole lot of well-intentioned advice. Some of it is quasi-medical, some superstitious, and some simply inane. Stand on your head after having sex. Dose yourself with cough syrup. Drink Tahitian Noni juice. Have sex every single day. Or every other day, or hardly ever except when you think you're most fertile. Although there are good kits available at most pharmacies to help you chart your ovulation and fertility peak periods, there's also something else you can try, something natural and absolutely free.

But first, let's review the basics of human conception. Ovulation occurs once per menstrual cycle. An unfertilized egg will live for approximately twenty-four hours. That's your whole window of opportunity. Daunting, isn't it? Sperm are even more fragile, temperamental sorts of players. Unless they are lucky enough to arrive during your peak fertility phase, those poor little swimmers will survive roughly two hours. Which is why it's incredibly helpful to know when fertility is at its peak.

There is a fairly easy way to become acquainted with *your* fertility cues. If you're prissy or uptight, brace yourself. This involves some hands-on body exploration. You may not realize that changes in the quantity and consistency of your vaginal mucus throughout the month are caused by naturally occurring hormonal shifts in your reproductive cycle. These changes, once you learn to read them, are extremely accurate signals that indicate whether or not you are in a fertile phase. During your cycle, as estrogen levels rise, the mucus will become more plentiful—you'll notice this as a slippery, or more lubricated sensation. This brings us to the hands-on part. Your fingers are the best means of gauging this mucus, though you can also use toilet paper if you just can't bear to deal with your own excretions. (Don't shudder and say, "Ew, gross!" Do you want to have a baby or not?) First you'll notice a sparse but fairly sticky kind of discharge. This is followed by a thinner, more cloudy or creamy mucus. In the final and fertile phase, the mucus will be thin, transparent, and very stretchy—kind of like the mucilage glue that weird boy in your first grade class liked to pour on his fingers, peel off, then eat. When you can grasp a bit of this mucus between your forefinger and thumb, and stretch it out—anywhere from one inch to four or more inches—then you are experiencing maximum fertility. All systems go! This stretchy mucus, which will remind you a bit of egg white, offers sperm maximum protection from the natural acidity of the vagina. It also helps propel the sperm along to its hoped-for destination: the outer wall of the fallopian tube where your egg awaits. In this hospitable mucus, the life span of sperm may even be extended up to three days, increasing your odds of fertilization. This method, by the way, is also used by many couples as a form of contraception. The Catholic Church actually teaches it, which is where I learned it. (Insert your own unplanned Catholic baby punch line here.) I used it to get pregnant with my second child—after a year of unsuccessful effort. Why didn't I use this method sooner? Because my first baby rendered me so exhausted and stupid that it never occurred to me, that's why. But when I was finally able to rub two brain cells together and remember to check my mucus, I got pregnant on the first try. Trust your body to know what it's doing—and be glad that my Olivia isn't running *you* so ragged that you can barely think.

maniac), I felt certain that we'd conceive our baby under a palm tree. Not so. Months went by, and every period was a crushing blow. I became a regular Lady Macbeth, all blood and gloomy pronouncements. It didn't help that everyone we knew asked us just about every day if we were pregnant. I began tiptoeing around the idea of myself as a forever-childless person. It was devastating. Just because I'd delayed having a baby didn't mean that I didn't want one. I wanted one desperately, and had put it off only so I could try and fix my screwy life. I thought I needed to do that to be a good mom. Was it too late? Had I traded a successful career in radio for motherhood? Would I have to make do with something else? Was a BMW or any other toy supposed to take the place of a baby in my heart?

I began seeing babies and pregnant women everywhere. It was like *Night of the Living Gestation.* Maternity clothes suddenly seemed so adorable. Toddlers were saucer-eyed little angels, spreading joy and merriment in their wake. There were babies in restaurants, at the movies, in the movies, on every TV channel, and in my dreams at night. Babies, babies, babies. Oh how I longed for one of my very own! An aunt ten times over, I prided myself on not having any illusions about kids. The piles of laundry they generate, the whining, the chaos! I knew that they were rife with germs and often gross or smelly. I knew that they spat and screamed and were sticky. I suspected that my baby would be every one of those things, and often all of them at the same time. Yours will be too, by the way. They all are. Even the babies who wear little Burberry rompers and Ralph Lauren caps are waste- and snot-producing machines. Deal with this: Your little precious will occasionally sport a crusty green mustache of petrified mucus—and you will become all but oblivious to it.

Before you have kids of your own, it's normal to find such creatures less than appetizing. If we dared to be completely honest, we would acknowledge that other people's kids can, in fact, be downright grue-some. Kids almost can't help but do repulsive things—innocently, unknowingly, but repulsive just the same. It's in their nature, part of how they explore and learn about their world. Just watching them eat, though, is enough to send some of us racing for the nearest rack of extra-strength condoms. It's wonderful that children are refreshingly honest, but extolling that fact makes for slim comfort if you're forced to witness one gagging a mouthful of half-chewed meatloaf back onto her plate. That's a spectacle so gross that only parents can watch it without a grimace. Of course, one day, you too will casually hold out your hand to catch a slimy morsel that your little one has decided to reject. You may already be wishing for the day. That's because when you're aching to be a mommy, even the kids with green gook dripping out of their noses seem less like tiny disease carriers and more like ail-ing lambs in need of a good cuddle. You know you're in trouble when the prospect of spending an afternoon with a pack of sugar-crazed toddlers who are swinging from the rafters at Chuck E. Cheese's strikes you more as impish fun than hellish torture. Those are the times when your arms feel emptiest, and there's nothing in the world that can fill them up but a baby.

In the midst of trying unsuccessfully to conceive, I happened to glance in the mirror and discovered that years of running and eating salad had finally paid off. Riddled as I was by the bugaboos of a repressed Catholic girlhood, even I could appreciate the state of peak fineness my body had attained. My Inner Nympho whispered, "Hey girl, let's go buy some slutty clothes." Why not, I thought, it's not like I'm pregnant. Might as well look trashy while I still can. Dragging my husband to the mall under this pretense, a treat for him since he com-plains that I dress mostly like a depressed Amish boy, I was deter-mined to leave garbed like a proper radio industry tramp. Inner

Nympho led us straight to Bebe. We pored through the racks of do-me attire, settling on an expensive pair of black leather pants. I tried them on, and, amazingly, they felt great. No wonder the women in head-banger videos looked so relaxed! They were soft, a little snug, and very sexy. They were also way too pricey. "They're an investment." My husband leered. "Get them. Get them in brown, too. Wear them home." So I did. Hey, a woman should listen to her man every once in a while, right?

Those pants are now hanging in my closet gathering dust. I wore them once, to be defeated by Rush Limbaugh for the 2000 National Association of Broadcasters Marconi Award. It was a difficult evening. I was deathly sick, crawling on my hands and knees in my room at the San Francisco Hilton, whimpering and begging, but it wasn't losing to Limbaugh that did me in. Nor was it a bad shrimp, too much wine, a virus, a microbe, or an evil eye. Apparently nothing encourages the reproductive process like having one's bottom sheathed in costly designer leather. The ink wasn't dry on the American Express charge slip before those pants were a waste of money.

Before you leap to the crazy conclusion that a pair of hot-looking leather pants turned my husband and me on to such a blazing degree that we couldn't help but conceive, please remember: This is reality, not a movie. There's a perfectly logical scientific explanation for my sudden leather-fueled fertility: The gods wanted to teach me a lesson about spending so much money on sleazy pants. The very act of slapping down my credit card, of breezily assuming that I, a nice Catholic girl, belonged in a pair of leather trousers instantly made me more fertile. It's the one theory that makes sense, and I'm not the only woman it's worked for. A listener swears that an even better way to get pregnant is to go hopelessly into debt for a two-seater sports car, preferably a convertible. She and her husband have one sitting idle in their garage, a staggering monthly payment, and a gorgeous eight-month-old baby boy. She's promised to take me for a ride in that car on the day I fit back into my leather pants—provided she can find a baby-sitter for little Dylan. Bottom line: If you want to get pregnant right now, go blow a wad of cash on something that only a childless person can use.

The Empress of Fertility

Your first pregnancy is truly a wondrous thing. Every sensation is new, every day brings fresh discoveries, and every person you know wants to share in your joy and anticipation. Bask in it. In fact, go ahead and wallow in it. Put your feet up and make all sorts of outlandish requests for things like fresh-squeezed limeade, out of season blueberries, white chocolate chip cookies, and the latest issue of *Glamour*. Be high maintenance. Require special handling, extra attention, and a great deal of fuss made over every pregnancy milestone. Enjoy yourself while you can, because your second pregnancy will be an entirely different experience. You will go from being the Empress of Fertility to being a gestational scullery wench—a veritable pregnant Cinderella. Your second pregnancy will be no big deal to anyone except you. Save yourself the trouble of future disappointment by preparing now for the reaction to *any* pregnancy after your first to be one of slack-jawed apathy, starting with the man who impregnated you and radiating outward to include the rest of humanity. Your first pregnancy is your one and only opportunity to lay it on thick—the nausea, the cravings, the insomnia, the bloating. Milk it for all it's worth. Try to at least get a decent piece of jewelry for your suffering. By the time you conceive baby number two, the novelty of seeing you with child will have completely worn off *and* you'll be frantically scurrying after baby number one. Better ask for a massage now, while you still can.

For extreme cases of sluggish fertility, there is one other technique you can try, though be warned that it's not for the timid or uncertain. It's called "debt and discord," and has been around so long that many of our own parents used it to conceive us. To work it successfully, you'll need to be in an unhappy relationship, one that seems to be headed for nothing but heartache. Add a hundred channels of cable television, a bong, and a refrigerator stocked with Coors. (This is all for your mate; the Misfit Mom is a role model for the healthy prenatal lifestyle.) Throw in some loud quarreling followed by protracted periods of icy silence. On the day that it seems you can take no more, your mate will come home and announce that he has been fired from his job. He will be so devastated that you will set aside your worries and offer him a round of consolation sex. As my friend Marsha, a veteran of "debt and discord," explained, "So there we were, miserable, broke, and he's drinking too much and unemployed. I knew I was pregnant the very instant it happened." Sure enough, her daughter Rachel arrived nine months later. It's not a perfect system, but Misfits know that nothing ever is. That's the secret of our resilience. And when it comes to making a baby in this vast and mysterious universe, sometimes miracles have to be coaxed.

3
The Pink Stick

There are few things in life capable of sending a girl careening from one end of the emotional spectrum to the other as dramatically as the home pregnancy test. Who hasn't slunk into the all-night drugstore to purchase one, praying all the while that stress, not a baby, is the reason for a missed period? Who hasn't felt flushed with relief at a negative result? Start trying to get pregnant, though, and that little plastic stick acquires a whole new kind of power. Those tests, which are designed to detect the HCG (human chorionic gonadotropin) present in a woman's urine after conception, are much more sensitive (translation: accurate) than they used to be. They also cost a bit less than they used to, which means that you can (and will) buy them in bulk. I once worked with a woman named Jody who used a home pregnancy test every morning. One day, after months of trying to conceive, she burst in to the conference room and trilled, "We're pregnant!" Amid many cheers and congratulations, someone asked, "How far along are you?" Jody happily reported, "About a week!" Cheap, accurate, easily obtained confirmation that yes, a human life is growing inside of you—it's not hard to see why the home pregnancy test can be as addictive as crack cocaine.

The particular test I always relied on featured two windows, with a positive result indicated by a pink line in both. All of my past windows had come up empty, so I was in no mood to stop by the store to buy yet another test on the night my husband suggested it. He was insistent: "You just ate a giant cheeseburger with bacon, barbecue sauce, and pickles. You've never ordered anything like that in your life. How could you not be pregnant?" He had a point. We spun a U-turn and zipped into the parking lot of a twenty-four-hour superstore. We dropped a bag of Twizzlers, a *National Enquirer*, and a home pregnancy test on the counter. Sensing the gravity of the moment, the cashier hefted the box, raised one eyebrow, and asked, "What are y'all hoping for?"

We drove home. I headed for the bathroom. Breaking the seal on the box, I suddenly realized that something was very different this time: I was nervous. It felt like the beginning of a roller-coaster ride when they've strapped you into a little car and sent it straining *click-click-click* up the track to the very top of what you belatedly realize is an insanely steep hill. I was giddy and queasy and thinking, "Stop. I've changed my mind. I'm too scared to ride." Then I ripped open the plastic bag, followed the directions, and closed my eyes. When I finally dared open them, adrenaline flooded my body, and my heart somersaulted in my chest. The stick was pink. Both windows. Free fall.

One of the unfortunate consequences of a wildly dysfunctional upbringing coupled with Italian Catholic guilt is the utter conviction that all of the bad things that happen to you are preordained and well deserved, while anything good that comes your way is a mistake. With this in mind, I immediately assumed that I'd purchased a faulty preg-

Pregnancy Lie Number one

Nine months . . . where exactly did we get *that* idea? Try forty weeks—that's the actual length of a human pregnancy. Let's work the problem together: If there are four weeks in a month, and forty weeks in a pregnancy, how many months does a pregnancy last? The answer is: ten. Pregnancy Lie Number One: Expect to be expecting for *ten* glorious months, not nine. Long as that is, it could be a lot worse. Elephants are pregnant for a whopping twenty-three months, camels for thirteen months, and if the killer whale had feet, she'd face the misery of swollen ankles for a solid year. Horses get off relatively easy with eleven-month pregnancies, though not so easy as that svelte water nymph, the hippopotamus. Her pregnancy is a mere eight months long. But for sheer efficiency, it's hard to beat the red squirrel. She can go from first date to first baby in just under six weeks. A six-week pregnancy! It's an insurance company's dream.

nancy test. It was only after buying and using six more that I began to think that there just might be something to seven consecutive positive results. Unlikely as it seemed that I could actually be someone's mommy, all the evidence was pointing in that direction. The time had come for an expert opinion. Off I went to the ob-gyn for a ride on the steel pony.

My doctor quickly confirmed the pregnancy, but, seeing my skepticism, sent for the ultrasound baton. (Note: While the thought of becoming intimate with any instrument described as a "baton" is unsettling, believe me, it's just the beginning of the increased traffic you'll be seeing in that area.) Within minutes I held in my hand a black and white printout of something that looked very much like a tiny beagle. My doctor helpfully wrote the word *baby* next to an arrow pointing at the beagle and sent me on my way with a big hug and a booklet full of useful information on everything from dietary guidelines to the size (a pear—the dreaded fruit analogy) of the average uterus. Once in my car I stared at that grainy and mysterious photo in wonder. Then I put my head on the steering wheel and had a good cry. It was really true: I was going to have a baby of my very own. The part of me that never believed it, the part that figured that becoming pregnant would be denied me, or would be as half-assed and cobbled together as everything else in my life, wept tears of joy and gratitude. But the rest of me, having spent thousands of dollars on therapy and countless hours on self-reproach, wept for the baby. What if I screwed it all up? My roller coaster had just plunged sharply into a curve. Poor little beagle with me for a mommy!

Welcome to pregnancy hormones. You'll be nuts. Know that now and plan for it. Issue warnings and disclaimers to all who surround you. Expect wide swings between joy and terror, anticipation and panic. Happiness may have pasted a permanent orgasmic grin on my face, but inside I was frantically taking inventory of every single time I'd gotten blotto in college. I'd also smoked a little marijuana back in the day, and popped the occasional Dexatrim or four to stay awake to study. Would my child be born with three eyes? Then there was the whole genetic issue to consider. My bloodline was laced with creepiness at best, outright mental illness at worst. Could any of it be hereditary? Given my motley lineup of ancestors, I seemed all but destined to have a child of below average height with a too-large head, a suspicious nature, a raging chip on its shoulder, and no aptitude whatsoever for math. Oh, and if a girl, virtually no lips. As the days of my first trimester flew by I became more and more convinced that only pigheaded denial could account for my selfish and ill-considered decision to breed. Was I mad to reproduce these genes?

When I wasn't cataloguing every criminally minded cousin, every talks-to-the-kitchen-canisters crazy aunt, I was intently focused on monitoring my newly wayward body. Any twinge, tickle, or pinch felt anywhere between my neck and my knees stopped me cold: Was the baby all right? Most of us, with the exception of professional dancers, athletes, and dedicated yoga practitioners, don't live in a heightened state of body awareness. We sort of pilot ourselves around like captains in charge of large freighters, focusing more on the big picture of our daily agenda than on the important but invisible work of the engine and boiler rooms. There's literally an entire world of activity inside the average body, and unless you're paying very close attention, you're bound to miss a lot of it. Until you find yourself with child. Then the body's many functions become a loud, insistent roar, demanding that you immediately stop whatever you're doing and gasp, "What was that?" I would have driven myself mad with irrational worries had I not been blessed with the ultimate pregnancy distraction: round-the-clock morning sickness.

It's not very reassuring to discover that no one seems to know why pregnant women get sick in the first place. The ever-villainous hormones are always named as the culprit, but you'll have a tough time finding an explanation more specific than that. Some experts say that progesterone slows down the digestive functions, and that having

---

Pregnancy Lie Number two

Morning sickness goes away by noon. The truth: not necessarily. Some women go through their entire pregnancy without so much as a burp. Others wake up each morning, have a dainty retch in the bathroom, and then take on the day feeling great. Still others, including we luckless Misfits singled out by the universe to endure endless trials, suffer ghastly nausea that knows no cure, *all day long*.

undigested food sitting in the gut causes the nausea and distress associated with morning sickness. Try telling that to a woman who's been able to eat nothing but flat Sprite and crackers for three days—she'll bite your head off.

Another interesting theory is that pregnancy sickness is a useful evolutionary tool, designed to prevent the expectant mother from eating anything spoiled, poisonous, or otherwise harmful to the developing fetus. If that's the case, it's one tool that was far more beneficial to the humans of old who lived in nomadic tribes than it is to the modern Misfit within easy driving distance of takeout Chinese and organic produce. And besides, what kind of sensible evolutionary strategy is it to have an expectant mother gag at the sight of a boneless chicken breast but gobble up an entire box of Count Chocula with gusto?

Real pregnancy books, along with well-meaning friends and acquaintances, will advise the eating of crackers, washed down with flat ginger ale. Every single person who tells you to try nibbling a cracker will do so in the tone of someone sharing a new and powerful revelation. You will be advised half a dozen or more times a day that crackers are the answer to your tummy troubles. Knowing this now may help you manage the feeling of hopeless frustration with which you'll soon greet the very word *cracker*. In fact, for me, crackers are synonymous with failure to this very day. Maybe crackers will actually work for you—good luck. I tried every brand of cracker made. Some were better than others, but all were functionally useless. The same applied to ginger ale. Bubbly and inoffensive as it is, it's a soft drink, not a carbonated miracle. When ginger ale failed to get the job done, I bought fresh ginger root and made my own healing brew. No good. I tried mint tea, bland broths, dry toast, flat Coke, Tums, Phillips Milk of Magnesia (a very sexy item to have perched on the bedside table), peppermint oil in hot water, ice packs on the back of my neck, aromatherapy, and New Age music. In a moment of desperation I even called on St. Jude, the patron saint of lost causes, to step in and offer some relief. Through it all I stayed as green and unwell as a poisonous toad.

Bad morning sickness feels like the worst motion sickness in the world combined with food poisoning and a voodoo curse. Certain smells make it worse, as do certain images, thoughts, and TV commercials, all of which suddenly feature big, greasy, leaking piles of revolting food. Your two goals at this stage of the pregnancy are: First, eat what you can, stay hydrated, and take your prenatal vitamins. Second, feel neither rage nor despair at being told for the hundredth time to nibble on crackers. Tolerating irritating but well-meant advice now is good training for the months to come when you'll be inundated with more of the same on every subject imaginable. Remind yourself that morning sickness can be viewed as an encouraging sign of a healthy pregnancy. This will make it easier to bear, though it can be a hard thing to remember while dry-heaving into a Porta-Jon at a city park.

To be deathly ill all day, every day, for weeks, then months on end may not break a woman's spirit, but it will erode her sense of style. I suspect this is nature's way of preparing a mom for how little time or energy she'll have to spare on frills like brushing her hair once the baby has arrived. Waking up at four A.M. to do morning drive radio didn't help matters for me. The alarm would go off—making whatever song was playing at that moment the barf anthem of the day— and I'd bang the snooze button and reach for a cracker. Only after choking one down could I even think about sliding to the floor and crawling into the bathroom. Getting dressed was a nightmare since I couldn't bear to have any clothing touch my violently rolling stomach. No matter that the fashion magazines exhort us otherwise, the grosser and sicker you feel, the grosser and sicker your style choices are likely to be. Mostly because you'll be too miserable to care. Hair and makeup were out of the question. It's hard enough to wield a blow dryer before dawn; it's even trickier when your head is in the toilet. Off I'd shuffle to work, pockets stuffed with Rolaids, clutching my thermos of useless ginger tea. Once there, I'd settle into my chair, turn on the microphone, and pretend that everything was fine.

Misfits do a lot of pretending; it's a skill we've honed over long years of practice. I concealed my illness because the possibility of miscarriage is highest in the first trimester of pregnancy. Used as I was to having things go wrong, I didn't want to tell anyone that I was pregnant until I made it through my third month. Most doctors encourage us to wait till that point before sharing our good news with family and friends. Even the sanest pregnant women will experience some anxiety in those first ninety days. It's perfectly normal. Misfits, however, are masters at rehearsing catastrophe. We mull all possible disaster scenarios, and then obsessively chew the juice out of every gruesome detail. We plan for and expect things to go terribly wrong. If they do, we're not surprised. Pain is familiar, chaos seems normal, and to us it only seems sensible to anticipate the worst. A Misfit thinks herself braced for just about anything—anything, that is, except pity. We hate pity. Pity makes us feel weak, vulnerable, needy, and out of control. Misfits crave control. We're prone to perfectionism, even arrogance. We like to go it alone, and are impatient with anything that defies or derails us. We're high-performance machines that were tooled and tested under the most demanding and unpredictable conditions: our childhoods. These attributes may have served us well then, but they can handicap us now. Anticipating tragedy forces us to live in a constant state of high alert. Pregnancy is the time to stand down.

Altering the way you approach the world is extremely difficult, but think of it this way: It's no harder than the work you've already done to get to this point. That's the beauty of the Misfit Way: All the really tough stuff is behind us. That's the good news. The bad news is, we're still wired for, well, bad news. That's why we're jumpy, worried, and unable to relax. Here's something tangible to try when the voices in your head are at their loudest, screaming all of the horrible things that are happening or are going to happen to you and your unborn baby.

Guess Where Your Face Is?

It's one thing to crawl around your own bathroom on your hands and knees, and quite another to find yourself sprawled out beside the employee toilet at work. Morning sickness can turn even a dream job into pure hell. Arriving at the radio station by five-thirty each morning gave me almost three hours of blissful barf privacy before the rest of the staff wandered in. But it wasn't total bliss—and here's why. We share a building with our sister station, an A.M. news/talk format populated almost completely by guys. Each of those guys spends the morning swilling down buckets of coffee and sprinting from microphone to men's room. If that facility happens to be occupied, the Bladder Boys simply commandeer the women's bathroom. Most days that wouldn't be a problem—after all, there's no such thing as cooties, right? One morning, though, gripped by a particularly dreadful wave of clammy nausea, I limped to the bathroom and found it locked. Ditto for the men's room. Faced with a brief wait or an undignified heave into a potted plant in the lobby, I opted for the former. Minutes ticked by. I could hear shuffling, water running. Finally the door opened. "Sorry about that!" boomed Co-worker X in his smoothest, most jovial voice. I ducked past him, collapsed onto my knees, and promptly lost my crackers. Kneeling there, my cheek resting on the cool porcelain rim, tears leaking out of the corners of my eyes, I gamely reminded myself that this was all a sign of a healthy pregnancy. Then it hit me: My face was parked in the same spot just vacated by Co-worker X's meaty rump. Morning sickness and work just don't mix—and when they do, it's never pretty for you.

Remember those elementary school fire drills where we learned what to do in the event our clothing caught on fire? It's called "stop, drop, and roll." Think of your mental catastrophe rehearsal as a fire, and your strategy to extinguish it as "grab, stop, and do." Grab your head with both hands and forcefully declare, "Stop." Say it out loud, no matter where you are. The physical action interrupts the mental churning. It forces you out of your head and back into your body, where sweating palms, a racing heart, and a cold sweat all signal anxiety. Stay out of your head and take a look around. Is there some actual threat in your environment, some real and definite danger, or were you screening a movie inside your head? Were you just imagining how utterly destroyed you would be by the loss of this pregnancy? Were you walking yourself step-by-step through the panic and horror and grief? Seeing yourself bleeding, the pained look on your doctor's face as she delivers the news? This is a classic dress rehearsal for catastrophe. Misfits slide readily into this behavior every single day, but pregnancy offers new and spectacular ways for us to terrorize ourselves.

The consequences of extreme anxiety extend beyond the emotional suffering we experience. The stress hormones that flood our bodies affect the development of our unborn children in ways that medical experts don't yet fully understand. Since our whole mission is to protect our kids from the kind of nuttiness we experienced as children, it makes sense to start right now while they're still in the womb. The first step is to stop the mental churning and return to the physical moment. It takes practice, and you may find yourself blurting "Stop!", grabbing your head twenty or more times a day—or even an hour. It is shocking to realize just how much of your life you've surrendered to panicky daydreams. But rehearsing catastrophe is like any other problem: You must be aware of it before you can resolve it.

The next part is easier because it offers Misfits the opportunity to exercise our greatest skill: control. Misfits are remarkable doers. We simply love to do things, and do them better than anyone else. We're driven to do. Fortunately, a whole new universe of doable things opens up for the pregnant Misfit. There are books to read and videos to watch. There are classes to attend. There are reams of new and necessary objects to be researched, selected, and purchased. Take a look around your house or apartment. If there's a project that needs tending to, this is the time. Once the baby comes, you'll be lucky to floss, much less paint the living room.

Understand this: A baby is a time- and energy-sucking vortex capable of defeating even the most organized and anal-retentive woman. Make a list right now of every single thing you'd like to accomplish. Include all of the ridiculous DIY projects you've seen on HGTV, as well as silly stuff like organizing your earrings, wallet, or junk drawer. Tape the list to the inside of a cabinet. Do NOT post it on the refrigerator or anywhere else that you might see it every day and feel overwhelmed by all of your chores. This list is going to help reduce your stress, not add to it.

Anxiety sneaks up on us, which explains why you might feel utterly relaxed and confident at dinner, only to be panicky and hysterical at bedtime. With pregnancy hormones working overtime as anxiety's evil henchmen, you not only won't see it coming, you won't realize that you're completely out of your mind until long after it arrives. Bedtime is particularly dangerous for the Misfit Mom-to-Be because sleeplessness plagues many pregnant women anyway. A pregnant, wide-awake Misfit is a catastrophe rehearsal waiting to happen. What to do? Perhaps our normal sisters happily count sheep in hope of drifting off. But when a Misfit tries to count sheep, the poor things wind up crashing into fences, getting their little legs lopped off, and, worse, turning into wolves. A sleepless and pregnant Misfit is an anxiety attack waiting to happen. Get out of that bed *NOW*. Practice your grab, stop, and do. March to the cabinet where you've posted your list of chores and projects, and select a task. Who cares that it's after midnight and you're sorting through photographs from your college days or surfing the Internet for cool maternity clothes? That's infinitely better than lying awake in bed with a pounding heart, envisioning tragedy. Your task will absorb and distract you. You'll also get something accomplished, which Misfits adore.

We may be women who've made the mistake of defining our worth by what we achieve as opposed to who we are, but by God, we're efficient. You've been putting this efficiency, this powerful drive to succeed, to work for others all your life. Make it work for you now. A color-coordinated linen closet won't solve all your problems, but it will help you manage some stress in the short term, and that's exactly what a pregnant woman needs. As for that missed sleep, don't worry about it. One, you sure weren't sleeping anyway there on your mattress of feverish imaginings. Two, you'll make up for it with drooling, dopey lunchtime naps and/or bouts of stone-cold unconsciousness on the couch at dinnertime. The only thing more tired than a newly pregnant woman is a hibernating grizzly bear and, truth be told, only a fool would stand between either one of them and a bed.

Perhaps the only thing you can reliably expect from your first trimester is for it to blow away every preconceived notion you've got about what it means to be expecting. From constant, wrenching nausea, to a baby that, at six weeks, looks more Snoopy than human, to panic-stricken freak-outs, pregnancy is a challenge. Having a baby is the most difficult physical feat that many women will ever experience. It's hard work. Inside your body, another human being is growing, changing, *becoming*. If you think of yourself as a cauldron in which life is stirring and sparking, it seems logical and right that you'd be exhausted or queasy or just a little bit wigged out. Pregnancy is so awe-inspiring and miraculous that pregnant women used to be worshipped as goddesses. Now we can't even get a seat on the subway, but back in our day we ruled this planet. That's the kind of respect and reverence we still ought to command. What we displaced Misfit goddesses are stuck with, though, is a hard-won appreciation of how messy and beautiful miracles really are. Just like us. Tell that to yourself the next time you're barfing. It echoes nicely amid all the porcelain in the bathroom, and it'll give you a much-needed laugh. Crackers, anyone?

4

You're a Big Girl . . . And Getting Bigger

Unlike unicorns, naturally beautiful women do exist. At least that's what the magazines would have us believe. Every woman I've ever met swears that she's a totally cosmetic invention, a walking example, as my friend Anne puts it, of better living through chemistry. I'm definitely in that category. On a good day, I tell myself that I could easily look worse. On a bad day, I feel more like a messy collection of magic spells and enchantments woven out of antifrizz hair serum, taupe eye shadow, and Maybelline Great Lash than I do a human female. There's no rolling out of bed looking radiant for me; I've got to put a little effort into it. Pregnancy presented a whole new set of challenges.

For starters, there's the much-promised gestational glow. I couldn't wait to get it, but thanks to my round-the-clock nausea, the glow emitted by my face was the greenish hue of radioactive waste. My hair changed too, though that probably had less to do with raging hormones than it did with my extreme lack of interest in brushing, blowing, or otherwise attending to it. Truth is, I was afraid to really look at myself in the mirror. What if hormones caused me to sprout whiskers or a mustache? What if I developed that weird facial discoloring I'd read about in all the books? It's called the "mask of pregnancy," which is a typically lovely pregnancy-book euphemism for what any sane person would clearly label a big, brown scary blotch. The correct medical term for this condition is *melasma*, which manages to sound both painful and potentially fatal, doesn't it? My friend Anne suffered temporary alopecia, otherwise known as baldness. She still hasn't forgotten (or forgiven) my horrified reaction to her vanishing hairline. ("You *gasped*," she says reproachfully. "You gasped at the sight of my head. Don't even try to deny it.") With these kinds of potential side effects, it can be challenging for a pregnant woman to feel her confident best. This is especially true in the final few weeks before delivery when your body feels ready to burst. Fashion gurus will cheerfully advise the wearing of bold jewelry or bright lip gloss to "draw the eye upward." Look, when you're carrying an extra fifty pounds between your neck and your knees, you'll need more than lip gloss to divert attention from your explosive girth. If you really hope to draw anyone's eye upward, you'll probably have to put an orange traffic cone on your head. As for me, I had extra cause for appearance anxiety, thanks, as usual, to my colorful upbringing.

My grandma Blackhair was a pro at guessing an unborn baby's gender. She didn't need fancy ultrasound or props of any kind. Her method had nothing to do with whether the baby was riding high up under the rib cage, or slung low under the belly. That kind of thing was for amateurs. She could tell just by studying the face of a pregnant woman, and I can't think of a single instance where she guessed wrong. "A boy will steal your beauty," she informed me, taking a long drag on her Merit Light. "It shows up in the face around month five. The nose changes shape and the whole face becomes distorted. You mark my words: An ugly face in pregnancy is a sure sign of a baby boy." I tried to argue with her, reasoning that it made much more sense for a girl to rob her mother of beauty, but she wouldn't hear it. "First of all, College Lips, everyone knows that a man will use up a woman's beauty till it's gone. They start in the womb. What, they didn't teach you that at your college?"

To illustrate this lesson in biology and gender politics, she pointed to my sister-in-law, Nancy. Pregnant with her fifth child, many days overdue, and lumbering around in the humid July heat like a belligerent rhinoceros, there was no denying that Nancy's face had changed. "It's a boy," Grandma Blackhair declared. "Look at her—she doesn't even look like the same person! It's terrible! It's a sin!" Like any woman who's gained seventy-five pounds, lost sight of her ankles, and been dubbed "Pregzilla" by her own husband, Nancy was delighted to have the family take such an interest in her altered appearance. Who wouldn't want to have her nose compared to a bell pepper? Who wouldn't enjoy hearing her face described in the kinds of biblical terms usually reserved for violations of the commandments? But right or wrong, kind or cruel, Grandma Blackhair's prediction was accurate, and Nancy delivered a healthy, gorgeous baby boy. (Note: Her beauty was restored soon afterward, as it always is once the marauding male child has exited the womb.)

Having successfully used the Blackhair Technique to predict infant gender for friends and coworkers, I can vouch for its accuracy, though not for your safety. It can be dangerous to tell a pregnant woman that her face has become hideously distorted. I made that mistake with a coworker seven years ago. Karen still isn't quite over it, despite having a very handsome little boy to show for her efforts. She repaid my kindness by scrutinizing me throughout my pregnancy, hoping no doubt to be the first to spot any developing horrors, and offering me frequent updates on my appearance. Frankly, I deserved it.

Waiting for my body to expand and my face to morph into that of a monster, I suddenly had a brilliant idea. Wouldn't it be fun to take some pictures of myself right now, wearing lingerie or a bikini, so that I'd have a little souvenir of my pre-baby body? My husband, having tried unsuccessfully for years to get me to agree to any sort of photo-related kinkiness, jumped right aboard this scheme. He was, however, a little taken aback by my sudden interest in exhibitionism. Like so many Misfits with weird body/sex issues, I tended to move through life as though I were a giant disembodied head, i.e., tripping over my own feet, avoiding mirrors, and swathing myself in funereal black garments. Getting those garments off had always been a real challenge for my husband. Now, confused and disoriented by this new request, frightened of my pregnancy hormones, and disbelieving his good fortune ("I'm going to take seminaked pictures of my wife!"), the poor man raced for the tripod. Thus was born The Home Soft-Core Porn Photo Shoot. Before you blush and say, no way, not me—or before you try to remember just who has those negatives of your first-ever public pole dance—let me explain. These pictures are going to pave the way for a body image epiphany that might just rock your perfectionist Misfit world. But first things first: You need a digital camera. Without digital, you'll have to take your film to be processed at a store, almost guaranteeing that quasi-erotic photos of you will fall into the sweaty hands of some random teenage miscreant who will eventually post them on the Web, where one day they'll come back to haunt you and sink your bid for Congress. Of course you've already considered this possibility, since being one step ahead of the game is a favorite Misfit survival strategy.

Next step: lighting. You want the finished product to resemble something Mario Testino shot, not a snap you'd find at the bottom of a pervert's favorite shoebox. While mood lighting is wonderful for seduction, it's lousy for photography. The same shadows that make your bedroom look enticing can make you look haggard and old. As a veteran of many professional photo shoots, I can promise you that you'll look fantastic when bathed in tons and tons of light. The light works to blast imperfections away, not reveal them. I always know that I'm going to love the finished photo if the light on my face feels like a roaring bonfire. So either switch on the lights or, even better, shoot outdoors late in the afternoon when the sunlight is rich and burnished. In Hollywood terms that's "the golden hour"—take advantage of it. Since when do you care what the neighbors think?

Next, pick out your favorite lingerie or swimsuit. Put on the makeup you wear normally, just a little darker on the eyes and lips. Think sex queen, not drag queen. Stretch out on the bed or chaise and try to remember the poses you've seen in the Victoria's Secret catalogs. Those babes don't just lie there like they're awaiting an autopsy. Shift your weight onto one hip. Bend the other knee. Lean on one bent elbow, while resting your other hand on the upper thigh of the bent leg. Tilt your chin slightly down, eyes up. Invite your man, who will be goggle-eyed and delighted at this display, to snap a few shots. Or you can ask your sister, your friend—someone you feel comfortable with—to help out. The great thing about digital photography is that it allows you to view the finished product instantly. Delete immediately anything that makes your jaw clench, but try to be objective. Look at your body in the same way you'd view a landmark or a natural wonder. Just like a tourist, you're taking a picture in case you never make it by this way again. (And you won't. This is your pre-baby body and, for better or worse, it'll soon be gone forever.) Adjust your pose, change the camera angle, snap away, and can you believe how fabulous you are? No? Don't worry. This particular exercise generally needs a few months to work its magic. Just trust me and take the photos, then put the disk in a safe place. You'll be glad you did once you arrive at your next destination. Welcome to Hugeville, population: you.

Gaining weight is so much fun at first! Especially if you've allowed

Stretch Mark Alert!

When it comes to the side effects of pregnancy, don't expect a whole lot of sympathy from anyone. The never-been-pregnant don't understand, the already-been-pregnant are secretly enjoying your suffering, and everyone else expects you to don the crown of mommy martyrdom and not be so endlessly focused on yourself. Which brings us to stretch marks: Is there any way to avoid them? Stretch marks happen when connective fibers in the skin's middle layer (or *dermis*) break. The areas most likely to be afflicted are the breasts, abdomen, thighs, upper arms, and buttocks. Forget buying any product advertised in the back of any magazine that promises to eliminate stretch marks. A prominent cosmetic surgeon assured me that there's not a blasted thing to be done to get rid of an existing stretch mark, short of surgical excision—and surely you're not that demented, right? You will note that pregnancy intersects perfectly with the aforementioned stretch mark zone—is there no end to the injustice visited upon females? While you may be a delicate little blossom destined to boast a zebra tummy for all time, there is something you can try that may save your skin. Pure shea butter, which is available by the pound on the Internet, is an amazing all-natural moisturizer. (Make sure to buy pure shea butter, not just a lotion that lists it as an ingredient.) Each day, rub a big dollop between your palms till it emulsifies, then generously coat your tummy, breasts, and bottom. You'll be slicker than a greased pig at a state fair, so you might want to save this particular beauty ritual for evening when you can swath your buttered body in a cotton t-shirt and pajama bottoms. I used shea butter daily, gained sixty pounds and four cup sizes, and walked away without a single stretch mark—and my skin is pretty fragile. Shea butter is also great for chapped lips, dry hair, and ragged cuticles—it's a multipurpose miracle product. I even used it to treat a particularly nasty diaper rash that Olivia acquired at four months. Pure shea butter is good stuff, and an excellent secret Misfit Mom weapon.

yourself to become a carbohydrate-avoiding, pleasure-denying, forever-dieting sinewy gym bone. Pregnancy feels like your invitation to eat anything you please, any time you feel like it. You can't wait for your tummy to bulge. You're in such a hurry to wear cute maternity clothes that you can hardly bear the excitement. Bring on that belly! In the first few months of my pregnancy, I rubbed my tummy so much you would have thought I was a statue of Buddha at a Chinese restaurant. I absolutely could not wait to start showing. Having lost a pound in my first trimester (see Pregnancy Lie Number One re "morning" sickness), I was anxious to give my baby everything it needed. As luck would have it, my rebellious stomach finally surrendered the fight and allowed me to eat on Thanksgiving Day. Finally, a reason to celebrate!

I started making up for lost time with a vengeance. Suddenly, food was delicious, incredible, intoxicating stuff, and I couldn't get enough of it. Not only did I want to eat, I wanted to cook! And the things I wanted to cook had names like Milky Way Bar Cake, Apple Brown Betty, Sinful Lasagna, and my complete undoing, homemade Double Fudge Ice Cream. Root beer floats for dinner? What a plan! I went from crying and gagging over a chicken breast to cackling with glee at the sight of a cheeseburger. It was madness.

Better Than Sex Cake*

1 box chocolate or devil's food cake mix
½ 14-ounce can sweetened condensed milk
6 ounces caramel ice cream topping
3 Heath bars, finely chopped
1 8-ounce container Cool Whip, thawed
1 complete lack of judgment or restraint on your part

*Not *always* better, but definitely easier for the very pregnant among us.

Bake cake according to package directions, using a 9 × 13 pan. Cool for five minutes on a wire rack. Using a paring knife, cut slits all over the top of the cake, being careful not to go all the way through to the bottom.

In a saucepan over low heat, combine condensed milk with caramel topping, stirring until smooth. Slowly pour this mixture over the warm cake, letting it seep into the slits. Sprinkle generously with chopped Heath bars.

Let cake cool completely. Frost with Cool Whip. Drizzle on more caramel topping (assuming you haven't already eaten what was left in the jar), and toss on some extra Heath bar bits for good measure. Refrigerate, then eat directly out of the pan.

Fat and calories: You're kidding, right? Let's just say *plenty* and leave it at that.

During this period, in which I assumed walruslike dimensions, I relied for strength on my patron saint of baby weight, the actress Catherine Zeta-Jones. I'd read somewhere that she'd gained eighty pounds while pregnant with her first child—eighty pounds! I figured that as long as I gained less than that, I was in great shape. That strategy became harder and harder to defend, what with her being a rich movie star who could hire people to smack the pounds off if need be, and me being the sort of person capable of driving to a quickie mart late at night to purchase the necessary ingredients for Better Than Sex Cake. But why be a downer? I was an honest-to-God barefoot, pregnant woman in the kitchen. It was glorious fun—even if the little Misfit in my head kept whispering, "You're gonna pay for this."

My mother expressed polite disbelief at my growing vastness. Her obstetrician had advised her to keep her pregnancy weight gain to an absolute minimum, using black coffee and cigarettes to control her appetite if necessary. That is so hilarious by today's health standards that it's like my OB suggesting that I reach for heroin instead of a bag of Pepperidge Farm Milano cookies. Black coffee and cigarettes. Caffeine and nicotine. Not that plenty of pregnant women today don't consume both, but it's not on the advice of their doctors.

Early in my pregnancy when it was all I could do to remain awake without gagging, my mother was puzzled by my endless fatigue, noting cheerily how energized she felt while carrying me. Granted, I might have been a big, lazy sloth, but maybe Chock Full O' Nuts deserves a little of the credit for her pregnant perkiness? Our mothers didn't obsess over nutrition, and neither, it would seem, did their physicians. They practiced the Back in the Day Pre-Natal Diet. What did they know about calcium, protein, and folic acid? No one understood that good prenatal care could prevent certain birth defects. No one comprehended the dangers of low birth weight. The smaller the baby, the easier the delivery, was the conventional wisdom of the time. Who knew then that low birth weight may have long-term health consequences or is linked to developmental delays? Face it: They didn't know anything.

Where we practically drown in helpful prenatal information from books and Web sites, even placards in city buses, our moms weren't entirely sure what was going on inside their swelling bodies. While we take something as simple as the home pregnancy test for granted, our young mothers knew no such ease or convenience. Ultrasound technology was the stuff of science fiction. In the absence of pictures, our mommies *had* to count our newborn fingers and toes to make sure that we'd come with all twenty. Relatively simple tests for such genetic abnormalities as Down syndrome or cystic fibrosis were unheard of. Much of what we consider routine treatment for infertility would have seemed absolutely, staggeringly miraculous thirty years ago. When you get right down to it, our mothers were practically cavewomen.

They copulated, became pregnant, and had babies. There were no in vitro fertilizations, no high-tech interventions. Mothers and babies were once in deadly jeopardy from the kinds of things that we can now take a single pill to correct—like Rh blood factor incompatibility. Childbirth claimed the lives of many women and babies—and this, remember, is circa 1960, not back in the dim days of *Little House on the Prairie*.

Two weeks before I was born, my mom was photographed looking slender and lovely, a glass of red wine in one hand, a lit cigarette in the other. I should have looked so good on my honeymoon. A few days after that picture was taken, she slipped on a set of icy stairs and took a bad tumble. Today we'd rush her to the hospital, slap a beeping monitor on her, and treat the pregnancy like an impending nuclear launch. Back then, she just picked herself up and brewed a cup of tea. No one panicked, no one obsessed, and if I have the story right, no one even came outside to help pull her to her feet. I asked her once, "Mom, do you think that I ended up kind of short and really stupid at math because of the coffee, cigarettes, and wine you had while you were carrying me?" Exercising her right as a mother to summarily dismiss my concerns, she rolled her eyes and replied, "You are so dramatic." Maybe. But I still wonder if the Back in the Day Pre-Natal Diet isn't responsible for stunting my growth.

Never having been anything quite so elegant as willowy or graceful, I was still unprepared for the sight of myself in the mirror. At seven months pregnant, there was no escaping the fact that I was just a blowhole away from landing a gig at Sea World. I was rotund, spherical, immense. My once B-cup breasts were now so large they were threatening to get a place of their own. My face wasn't hideous yet, but there was still time. And my nose was always runny.

You will not feel like the supremely confident fertile earth mothers whose photographs grace your pregnancy books. Those women, hands cradling their gleaming bellies, eyes gazing dreamily off into the distance, are fiction. They represent an ideal—the pregnant woman as a sort of benevolent, beaming, baby-making Crock-Pot. Other fictional ideals include the Rachel character on the television show *Friends*. On a hot summer day, her baby long overdue, Rachel arrives on the scene wearing a tiny midriff-baring tank top and a skirt riding low on her hips. She is wearing rings on her non-puffy fingers and is walking about on non-swollen ankles. She's cranky, but still adorable and sexy. This is make-believe and not at all representative of reality. I have never seen nor met nor even heard of a real past-term pregnant woman who looked fabulous in a belly shirt. Right now

Pregnancy Lie Number three

You're only pregnant from the neck down. Pregnancy hormones affect all mucous membranes, and may cause swelling and puffiness. This is why pregnant women can be what the literature terms "a bit stuffy." That's in a perfect world. Here in the real world where many women rely on antihistamines or prescription medications to control allergies, those swollen membranes are ghastly. Pregnant women can't take most medications, leaving us dripping and sneezing for nine months, with an alluring nasal twang to our voices. And while we're on the subject of mucous membranes, here's a Pregnancy Fun Fact: Your gums will probably bleed. That's right, after a long day of heaving around your now-enormous bulk, stopping periodically to weep at the sight of a puppy or a diaper commercial, you'll brush and floss your teeth (assuming you can find a brand of toothpaste that doesn't make you gag), only to transform the bathroom sink into a crime scene. There will be nights when you will brush, bleed, gag, then creep wearily to bed feeling big, weepy, and defeated.

you're thinking, but *I* will, and I'm laughing *ha ha ha*, because I said the same thing. All control-freak perfectionist Misfits do.

Have the courage to face the truth: The odds of an extremely pregnant woman looking terribly chic are slim. Brace yourself to look less like any (pick one) pregnant actress or supermodel, and more like my friend Marsha. In her last weeks of pregnancy, Marsha practically lived in a blue-green floral sundress, the only garment she owned that didn't cause her to swelter in the early summer heat. The result? She resembled the earth as seen from space. Perhaps the best a realistic Misfit Mom-to-be can hope for is to have her roots done a few days before she goes into labor, and maybe a pedicure. Why set the bar any higher? It only creates stress at a time when extra stress is the last thing you need. In fact, to encourage good mental health, the wise Misfit should avoid any and all publications that feature fawning articles about celebrity pregnancies. Those women live a fantasy of personal chefs, trainers, housekeepers, and other assorted minions from stylists to feng shui consultants. The delightfully unrealistic example they set is a hazard for Misfits who not only need to do everything right, but also look their best while doing it.

Remember the breathless news reports detailing how America's most famous Misfit Mom, Madonna, visited a salon for hair color and a manicure just prior to delivering her second child? I recall being not only impressed by the Material Girl's maternal priorities, but inspired by them—now *that's* a woman who knows how to take care of herself. A Misfit will seek to control as many variables as she can, starting with herself, then working her way toward everything and everyone else. We hate to be sloppy, because sloppiness leads to chaos, and chaos is something we've had enough of. But pregnancy is messy. Motherhood is chaotic. What's a pregnant Misfit to do if she wants to avoid becoming a *Mommie Dearest*?

Ten Left-Handed Compliments and Thoughtless Remarks Routinely Offered to Pregnant Women

1. You must be enjoying having such thick, shiny hair for a change.
2. *All that weight* will probably come right off once the baby is born.
3. A baby will give you something other than yourself to think about.
4. You look so different now that you have breasts.
5. Don't worry—no one expects a pregnant woman to look really good.
6. You'll finally get some use out of those childbearing hips.
7. So what if your nose has gotten wider—no one's looking at your face.
8. You don't look nearly as big from behind.
9. It must be hormones that make your skin all blotchy like that.
10. Somebody's been eating for two!

I had a great therapist who helped me understand that I would always be a perfectionist, that I would always struggle with extravagantly high expectations for myself, but that I could learn to recognize and manage the tendency. That's our task. You see, when a Misfit is instructed to learn to love and accept herself, she attacks that mission with gusto, often ending up in a tailspin of self-reproach over her failure to become Gandhi. Only we could twist counseling into an opportunity for yet more nuttiness. That's because perfectionism is more than a bad habit; it's a way of confronting the world, an orientation toward reality that is ingrained in a Misfit and resistant to change. But change is possible, starting with the expectations we have for ourselves. All our lives we've been the girls who take care of business, who get it done fast and right, at whatever cost to our own needs, wishes, or peace of mind. Forget that. The path to real happiness seems to have been far better marked out by those women whose attitude is a whole lot closer to screaming, "Kiss my ass and do it yourself, sweetheart." They may seem at first glance to be self-centered divas, but that's a misconception. We Misfits can learn a lot from their queenly example. Since pregnant women are expected to display a certain amount of serve-me-I'm-special attitude anyway, this is a good time to practice letting go of our need to fix every single problem, person, or life that gets dumped in our now shrinking laps. The mantra of the recovering Misfit is KMADIY.

We can begin managing our perfectionism by prioritizing the things we feel we absolutely must do in order to remain sane, then giving ourselves permission to do those things without anxiety or remorse. This applies to everything from volunteering to save the rain forest, to cleaning out the closets, to waxing your eyebrows. If motherhood is the mother of all battles (sorry) against perfectionism, pregnancy is our boot camp. Break yourself down to basics, starting with the easy stuff, like grooming. For example, I couldn't care less about nail polish, but am driven mad by two-tone roots. So I waddled to the salon and had my hair colored five days before my due date. A listener confided that her legs were as furry as a Sasquatch by month nine, but she never missed a manicure. The goal is to acknowledge what you need and why you need it, then do it without apology, explanation, or guilt. Sounds easy, but for the Misfit who has spent her life trying to justify her needs, her wants, her very existence, this is a high hurdle to jump. Having earned our way in the world by being superdriven and reliable, we're afraid that if we loosen the reins even a bit we'll disappoint the people we care about, and risk losing our place completely. With our self-hating, neurotic perfectionism cleverly disguised as efficiency and ambition (hello, Martha Stewart!), we've created seemingly enviable lives. That we're never satisfied with those lives is our secret, one that breeds only more discontent and feeds the endless cycle of expectation that there is something we ought to be doing differently or better.

Now comes baby to make the perfect picture complete. Except, your feet hurt. Your back aches. Your weight is creeping toward a number that would qualify you to play high school football. You've been studying your weaknesses and flaws, and the list keeps growing. You're so tired all the time—how will you ever find the energy to take care of a child? You feel barely able to take care of yourself these days. And what was that strange, fluttery sensation? Could that be the baby? There it is again! A baby, an infant, an actual human being is swimming around inside your body! It's too exciting! You can feel your baby! But what were you thinking, bringing a child into this totally vile and screwed-up world? What on earth will you do with a baby? What if it wails and howls and refuses to sleep? What if you can't handle the responsibility? But there it is again, a faint twinge, a curious, liquid sort of tickle that freezes you in place while you wait and hope for another signal from your tiny and mysterious passenger. My baby, you think, mine, and then you start to cry, something you do a lot these days. Go ahead and indulge in a good, long, weepy fit. Happy tears, worried tears, scared-to death I'm-not-perfect tears— just cry it out for now. Then blow your nose and come on—there's nesting to be done.

5

Do As I Say and Nobody Gets Hurt

In their first months on earth, babies don't need much of anything to get by. Loving parents, a warm, safe place to sleep, milk, cozy pajamas, and some diapers—that's pretty much it. All the other stuff we do for them—the fabulous nursery, the Italian crib, the piles and piles of sweaters, booties, plush toys, blankets, books, murals, mobiles, and musical battery-gobbling thingies—that's for us. Toil all you like over your hand-painted Humpty Dumpty wall borders, but understand that your baby might as well be on the moon for all it matters to him or her.

If we had any sense, we'd save our money and energy and wait to go hog-wild on the decorating till our babies were three or four years old. But we don't and we won't and there's a perfectly good biological reason for it. Scientists have termed it the *nesting instinct*, which calls to mind a plump mama duck settling her oversize bottom onto a clutch of warm eggs—not an image readily embraced by the modern woman. It sounds quaint and homely, like something our grandmothers were stuck with, but that we've outgrown. None of us outgrow biology, though, and the urge to nest overtakes the pregnant woman in a big way. Some of us become insane clean freaks. One woman I know, retired from the Air Force and the vice president of a major company, described cleaning the baseboards in the baby's room on her hands and knees over and over—and being unable to sleep till the job was finished to her satisfaction. Others become total product queens, frantically searching the Internet for the latest Peg Perego stroller, and name-dropping the latest fad baby brands ("Wait till you see the darling little biker jacket I just found at Rock Star Baby!"). The Misfit Mom-to-be is in her glory during this stage, since there is no one better at organizing and assaulting a project. The Misfit not only loves to *do*, she shows her love by doing. For the Misfit, nesting isn't just an instinct; it's a blissful orgy of accomplishment.

I thought I was pretty bad. First I succumbed to the outrageously expensive baby furniture. Then came the velvet cheetah crib bedding—velvet, of all things, for a creature famed for leaks and eruptions of all kinds. I knew it was crazy, but I was powerless to stop

Pregnant at Work, Radio-Style

We were scheduled to fly to an affiliate market for a day of appearances. As is customary in radio, things started going wrong early. Luckily, I was five and a half months pregnant, and just uncomfortable and hormonal enough to enjoy every minute of it. The day began with the news that the plane was broken—always an auspicious beginning for nervous fliers like me and my radio partner, Bob Lacey. Two hours later a substitute plane arrived: an eight-passenger jet with the name "Memphis Belle" emblazoned on its side. Another good sign, what with the original Memphis Belle being little more than winged hope held loosely together with rusty bolts. We boarded and strapped in for the brief flight to Fayetteville, North Carolina. In keeping with the day, there was a nasty spring thunderstorm hovering over our destination. Our Memphis Belle lacked some sort of gyro-stabilizer thingy, which meant that the strong winds tossed and pitched it about like a cheap canoe. (I should have paid more attention when the pilot explained all of this but I was near death from airsickness at the time. We landed, and I wobbled off in search of a nice quiet bathroom to barf in. There was no one waiting to meet us at the airport, which seemed odd. Turned out that our affiliate station had rented a brand new Ford Expedition to ferry us around in, with the night deejay—let's call him Kid C.—as our driver. Kid stopped off at a convenience store to pick up some lunch and left the keys in the ignition of the Expedition. Not surprisingly, Kid then stood on line in the store and watched as thieves drove away in his borrowed ride. Eventually, the general manager of the station came to fetch us, full of apologies and so much good-natured optimism about the whole event that Bob and I made a note to find out what he was taking so that we could get some, too. Best of all, another station employee showed up just then with lunch: sandwiches from the infamous car-jack convenience store. As I studied the gray-pink ham that seemed mostly gristle and the bright orange cheese-like slab that accompanied it, both nestled between slices of damp white bread, the baby kicked. Even the unborn know botulism when they see it. And, contrary to what you may have heard, pregnant women *won't* eat absolutely anything you put in front of us. Even we have our standards. I made do with a stray Twizzler I found in my purse and congratulated myself yet again for having risen to a position of such dazzling show business glamour.

myself. We painted the house inside and out, replaced countertops in the kitchen. Wait a minute—what do counters have to do with babies? The answer is: Nothing! Nothing at all! But the nesting instinct doesn't discriminate. It takes over your whole life.

Our funky safari nursery became my driving obsession. I drove all over town looking for the perfect leopard-print bath mat. I searched the Internet for purveyors of faux animal skin throw pillows and picture frames. We ordered drawer pulls in the shapes of rhinos, hippos, and elephants—beasts I felt a new sympathy for as I hauled my gigantic body in and out of hardware and furniture stores. (By the way, for what we paid for those drawer pulls, I believe we could have purchased the actual animals themselves.) I prowled through flea markets, antique shops, baby boutiques, and decorating centers in search of just the right wastebasket. My baby's dirty wipes wouldn't land in any old random receptacle! Every single thing we put in her nursery was disinfected first, then placed, re-placed, and placed again till it was perfect. Housework had always been my enemy, but I cleaned every inch of that room, even going so far as to take a Q-tip to the windowpanes.

Plumping pillows, rearranging teddy bears, adjusting lampshades, I'd daydream about what it would be like to have a real live baby nestled in that luxurious crib—a baby that would gurgle and coo and no doubt look smashing in a wee knitted jumper. Too bad it wasn't completely perfect there in my fog of giddy nesting. There was that little Misfit voice whispering, "You're out of control, you're a revolting yuppie cliché, you're nuts—wait a minute—are you sure those sheets are soft enough?" I feared I'd gone too far—and then I heard Debbie's story.

Debbie called our radio show one morning and described her baby's nursery. For starters, she spun and dyed her own yarn, then wove a rug to line the floor. She then stenciled and hand-painted a mural featuring all of the most famous nursery rhyme characters. While that was drying, she made a darling little lampshade and a matching picture frame. Then she designed, cut, and sewed curtains, crib bumpers, sheets, and a quilt. I'm pretty sure that she also made and painted her own changing table and shelves. Oh, and she whipped up a night-light, too. This woman tore through that room like some demented Martha Stewart on acid, creating a one-of-a-kind nursery that was sure to elicit gasps of wonder. The room screamed, "Look at what mommy did for you!" Here's the really terrifying part: She had two other kids and a full-time job, making her possibly the most over-achieving Misfit Mom ever. She was a working, gestating, weaving, stitching, stenciling, nonsleeping, super craft queen machine. I asked her why she'd gone to such extremes—I mean, come on: Weaving your own rug? Who does that? Her answer laid it all bare: "I had to do it so my baby would know how much I love her."

And there it is. The Misfit associates love with action, believing that she can earn love only by doing, not by being. In fact, she's made her-self into a human whirlwind precisely to distract others from seeing the worthless person she believes she really is. (Incidentally, this is why some of us have labored so long on the pointless task of trans-forming unworthy frogs into princes, or in my case, "artists" into taxpayers. Misfits enjoy a project every bit as much as we love a chal-lenge.) Raging nursery insanity is actually a very simple form of over-compensation: *I* never had a princess bedroom with collectible dolls, ballerina wallpaper, and a canopy bed, but *my* little girl will.

The problem with using material objects to wreak vengeance on the past isn't just that it can be so expensive and tiring. Flinging pricey European toys and crib linens at our own inner psychic pain doesn't offer a truly lasting cure. Shopping, painting, decorating, and rear-ranging provide a temporary high at best. As soon as the thrill of acquisition wears off, we're left with a pile of bills and a nagging emptiness, like hunger, only less easily satisfied. And if you're count-ing on big kisses and awestruck appreciation from your baby, forget it. Babies take everything for granted—from Q-tips, to Donna Karan blankets, to the constant and steady presence of mommy. A baby can't thank you for all of your generosity or unselfishness, and mommies who expect that are due for either a) an unpleasant awakening, or b) a lifetime of harping bitterness interrupted only by bouts of melodramatic guilt infliction.

When the Misfit says, "Look what I did—now will you love me?", she's equating love with payback. That's how she finds herself running on an emotional treadmill, never getting anywhere but exhausted. All my sacrifices! All my hard work! For you! I do it all for you! Desperate to prove herself loveable, the Misfit keeps upping the ante until even she, with her Herculean powers of management and ingenuity, can't top herself and ends up a cringing hag strewing guilt and recrimination in her wake. Don't let this happen to you. Please don't become that woman. You know her, you despise her—maybe you even want to strangle her. You sure didn't want to call her very often, or spend much time with her, or engage in any activity that wasn't an absolute duty when she was *your* mother, did you? Break the cycle right now. Your baby is your best hope for redemption because that baby arrives in the world with the one thing that can reform you: unconditional love.

The great and glorious news about babies is that they love us just because we're their mommies. They adore us no matter how clumsy, inept, sloppy, or untalented we may be. They love us if we're overweight, not particularly beautiful, or up to our ears in debt. A mommy doesn't have to be smart, pretty, successful, or perfect in any way. Just being mommy is enough. Don't believe it? Look how much we loved *our* mothers, and they made all sorts of mistakes with us. Some were absent or negligent. Some were overbearing or judgmental. Some were openly cruel or abusive. Some just weren't up to the task of caring for us or, worse, were fundamentally incapable of loving us. And none of it mattered, because we loved them with all our hearts anyway. The love a child feels for her mother is as awesome a gift as it is a responsibility. That doesn't make it okay to lock your kid, who will love you no matter what awful thing you do, in the bathroom so you can go out drinking with some skanky guy you picked up at the bowling alley. It simply means that you don't have to campaign for your child's love. You get it automatically. No one will ever love you like your baby, even if all you do is show up each day and hold out your arms. So relax.

Admit that the elaborate nurseries we contrive for our babies are really for us. There's nothing wrong with that. Nesting is a fun, joyful part of pregnancy, and allows us to explore our creativity. You don't need to make excuses, especially when you consider how many of us spent our first nights on earth wedged in a dresser drawer. At least that's what your mother will claim the first time she lays eyes on the gauzy canopy of silk, accessorized with sparkling rhinestone fireflies, that encircles your baby's crib. "A drawer was good enough for you," she'll mutter. And it was. Remember, when we were born, babies were the things that sexually active people ended up with. Our parents never dreamed that babies would one day be the focus of a multimillion-dollar apparel and furniture industry, much less that any rational person would spend buckets of money on frills like a cashmere receiving blanket. Don't get me wrong—I love cashmere. But then, I don't spontaneously regurgitate all over myself, or at least I haven't since college. Cashmere isn't for swaddling babies, unless you're so fabulously wealthy that you also plan to diaper your little munchkin with crisp twenty-dollar bills.

Merchants go fishing for your money, using your baby and your incipient Misfit Mommy guilt as the bait. Don't bite. Be particularly disdainful of magazine articles featuring celebrity moms and their pampered tots. Just because So-and-So Television Star only allows her little angel to suck on binkies made from organic rain forest rubber harvested by authentic vegan nomads is no reason for you to rush to do the same. Spending excessively and piling heaps of goods onto a helpless infant is just another way of trying to earn love by doing. It's crazy, unnecessary, and destructive. You end up with an empty bank account, a spoiled little tyrant, and worst of all, a gnawing feeling of status inadequacy that will make you frantic. Is a designer label worth all that? If you find yourself swooning over a silk Dior romper just because it is so damn precious and you must have it now, firmly remind yourself that the intended recipient of this luxurious garment *will* poop on it. Let's hope that gives you the strength to flee the store with your wallet intact.

The only exception you are obliged to make is in matters of safety. Buy the best-rated car seat you can afford. Ditto for high chairs, playpens, and other baby-containment devices. A baby is a cunning little Houdini, capable of figuring out every sort of buckle, strap, zipper, and latch. Don't make it easy. We chose a car seat that employs more straps, fasteners, and restraints than OSHA mandates to protect riders of inversion roller coasters. It's both massive and intimidating. I'd never seen anything like it—and why would I? None of us had car seats. Heck, most of us never even used a seat belt until high school driver's ed. Ask older women how babies traveled back in the day and you'll hear everything from "on my lap in the front seat" to "in a clothes basket" to my personal favorite, "rolled up in a towel and crammed behind the driver's seat." As someone who treats a good leather handbag with more kindness, I ask you: Were our parents baboons? It's a wonder we survived to breed at all.

In between bouts of painting and shopping, you'll be reading books on pregnancy and childbirth, and you will despair. Although these books are packed with useful information, they are also packed with wholly new and terrifying things to worry about. That's because pregnancy is a difficult and sometimes dangerous undertaking, a fact that we embrace on the one hand—witness the state-of-the art neonatal units at many large hospitals—and gloss over on the other, i.e., many workplaces still treat pregnancy as a selfish move on the part of women to cheat the boss out of a few bucks. I don't care how pragmatic and unimaginative you are, reading about Everything That Can Go Wrong while under the influence of hormones will turn you into a fearful basket case. In fact, at right about the eighteenth week of your pregnancy, you will stumble across the chapter on molar pregnancy and nearly have a nervous breakdown. A molar pregnancy, or *gestational throphoblastic disease*, is essentially an abnormality of the placenta at fertilization. There are two kinds: in the first, the nucleus of the egg is missing, leading to a placenta without an embryo. That's the nightmare: All of the symptoms of pregnancy minus the baby. In the other type, the fetus has so many chromosomal abnormalities that it almost always dies in utero. A molar pregnancy can also become a form of cancer, which, though treatable, can jeopardize your future fertility. Any Misfit worthy of the name will be instinctively drawn to information like this, which is why a pregnancy book can be a real minefield for us. They're full of new catastrophes just waiting to be rehearsed.

All of this research will coincide with your first ultrasound, an event that seems like a happy opportunity to discover whether you'll be delivering an Adam or a Zoe but which instead turns out to be a day fraught with the possibility of learning that something is wrong with your baby. And the frightening truth is, things do go wrong. In fact, when you think of what is happening inside your body, the cells dividing and replicating, the genes turning on and off, certain cells becoming bone and others spleen, heart, and liver, it's a miracle that most babies are born perfect and whole. When presented with reams of pamphlets explaining the many genetic and diagnostic tests available to me, the newly pregnant human, I was overwhelmed with all that could be learned from a series of relatively painless blood tests. Boggled, I asked a nurse how I should decide which tests to take and which, if any, might be unnecessary. She thought about it for a moment and replied, "I'd do every single thing my insurance company would pay for." Spoken like a true American.

Unfortunately—and scarily—even the most sophisticated tests can be misleading or inaccurate. For example, results of the alpha feto-protein (AFP3) test, which screens for genetic abnormalities and open neural tube defects that can indicate spina bifida or Down syndrome, are calculated using the mother's age as a factor. (Neural tube defects have been linked to inadequate amounts of folic acid. Take your prenatal vitamins!) Meaning, the older you are at conception, the greater your chances of having what's called a false positive. This is really a misleading term, since the test is not designed to yield a definitive positive or negative result. Rather, the test measures three specific hormones, then compares your hormone levels and age to hundreds of thousands of other pregnant women's levels and ages to come up with a statistical probability. This statistical prediction is all an AFP3 can give you, which is why a "good" result, i.e., one showing a low statistical probability for Down syndrome, is no guarantee that the baby is normal. What may make the AFP3 scary is how dramatically the odds can turn against you after age thirty-five. Example: A woman I know had test results indicating a 1 in 893 chance of genetic abnormalities at age thirty-three. At age thirty-nine, her AFP3 test results indicated a 1 in 89 chance. Which leads us to the following Misfit Mom question: Why take a test that doesn't really provide a straight answer and may in fact cause you to hyperventilate unnecessarily?

The AFP3 test is often done in conjunction with the very exciting level II ultrasound, both of which are meant to help you and your doctor gather information about your developing baby. Neither of the above procedures are invasive, and they pose no risk to you or your baby. However, an abnormal ultrasound or a positive AFP3 result may steer you straight in the direction of amniocentesis, a test that *will* provide definitive answers. Amniocentisis involves inserting a long needle directly into the amniotic sac while you and your baby lie there and watch helplessly. As useful and comprehensive as it is, no pregnant woman has ever relished the thought of having amnio, and since the test does carry a small but legitimate risk of causing miscarriage, it's not a procedure to be undertaken on a whim. Amnio is serious medicine, but it's not a mandatory test. The choice to use it—or not—is yours.

While pregnant with their first child, my brother and his wife suffered a terrible blow when their doctor informed them that tests indicated that their baby was a likely candidate for a genetic disorder called Trisomy 13. Trisomy 13 occurs in roughly 1 of 20,000 births, and three quarters of all Trisomy 13 babies die within their first year. Stunned by this tragic diagnosis, they sought a second opinion. More tests (including amniocentesis) and weeks later, they were told, "Never mind. False positive. The baby's fine." They didn't dare believe it until they held their newborn daughter in their arms. My sister-in-law, a Misfit if there ever was one, is still a little shaky—and that was eight years ago. The same thing happened to the wife of a coworker, right down to the "never mind" phone call three weeks after their nightmare began. Knowledge may be power, but it only takes a little bit of knowledge to fuel a Misfit Mom-to-be maternity meltdown. Still, for all the new flavors of anxiety modern medicine can deliver, would we ever want to trade places with our own mothers?

Those poor things didn't know if they were having a boy, a girl, or a three-headed squirrel until the moment of truth in the delivery room. It's better to live by the maxim that the only time during pregnancy that ignorance is truly bliss is when the subject in question is your weight.

Is there anything a Misfit can do to ease some of her prenatal anxiety? Definitely. Focus on caring for yourself and your baby. You're a genius at setting goals and figuring out requirements; use those skills to turn your pregnancy into a mission. If you haven't already, quit smoking. Don't roll your eyes—since when are you one to make selfish excuses? You can deal with nicotine withdrawal much more easily than your baby can deal with nicotine addiction. Cut back on caffeine. Make sure that you're getting plenty of calcium and protein. Get more rest. No, seriously—find a way to get more rest. After asking my OB if she had any theories as to why, in my first trimester, I had such a pronounced desire to kill another human being with my bare hands, I was told that fatigue is a leading cause of moodiness in pregnant women. I had to believe her. A nap seems a small thing, but if it stops you from committing a homicide then it's worth penciling one into your busy day. Keep exercising—it really does make a difference, not only in the delivery room, but afterward when you're anxious to return to your prebaby shape.

Embrace your pregnancy as the once-in-a-lifetime opportunity it is for both you and your child. Instead of desperately rushing to please others, you have the ultimate excuse to simply take care of yourself. Given the Misfit predilection for martyrdom, most Misfits require permission to be what they perceive as weak. Pregnancy grants that permission—it's an actual note from your doctor saying, rest, relax, and put yourself first. That last is difficult for the Misfit who wants always to please and accommodate others. Don't waste this opportunity to loll about like grand gestating royalty. Believe me, after the baby is born you'll be right back to your old tricks, outdoing and outperforming everyone—and with a baby you'll have virtually no diva time.

If you need further incentive to calm down and take it easy, think of the impact your good prenatal choices can have on your child. I'm not referring to the practice of blasting Beethoven at your belly; though if you feel like doing that, by all means knock yourself out. See yourself as a construction site. You are building a baby, cell by cell, inch by inch, and your baby deserves the very best tools and materials you can provide. There's a challenge worthy of any Misfit Mom-to-be. Just be prepared for weirdness. I'd spend a day carefully nibbling on steamed broccoli, turkey, and low-fat milk, only to end up in front of the refrigerator later that night guzzling the brine out of a jar of green olives—my own special mommy martini. I talked to one mom who couldn't stop eating uncooked dried pasta, and another who gobbled maple syrup by the spoonful. Pregnancy cravings vary and you may never experience a single one. But if you do, go ahead give in a little. If your upbringing didn't kill you, eating a chocolate-frosted doughnut won't either. Besides, don't you absolutely despise those women who virtuously deny themselves every imaginable indulgence? Is it their mission to make the rest of us feel like out of control cows? No one is recommending that you scarf down a bucket of Cool Whip, but let's don't be prissy about a few M&M's.

Painting, shopping, reading, fretting, and eating—that's a pretty full day for anyone. For the growing-ever-larger pregnant Misfit who is still expected to show up for work, manage a household, and remain fascinating to her man, it's starting to feel like a burden. It doesn't help matters that your once reliable and strong body is starting to protest being dragged off the couch. It wants to nap and watch decorating shows on HGTV, not buy groceries or fold laundry or go to meetings.

This body, the one you thought you knew so well, has begun to misbehave. Why, just the other day you glanced at a reflection in a shop window and felt pity for the graceless creature waddling toward you. Then you realized exactly who that poor waddler was: It was you. Pregnant women don't slink down the sidewalk like runway models. We waddle. We also lumber, and occasionally—if our feet are hurting—we shuffle. It's far from sexy, but it isn't shameful either. Stick a big watermelon down the pants of any typical biped and she (or he) will develop a bit of a side-to-side gait, too. It's just the way it is. Don't be disheartened to discover that your stride has more in common with an arthritic bear than it does a ballerina. It's usually not permanent.

Another temporary condition you may experience has no formal medical name, though it is sometimes casually called *My Pregnant Wife Is Such a Bitch, But If I Complain I'm a Rat Bastard*. This syndrome is easily identified by the following behaviors:

1. **Thermostat Suspicion.** As in, "I'm sorry, have we invited Satan to dinner? Is that why it's so hot in here? Open a window before I suffocate. I think I'm going to pass out. I know you turn the heat up when I'm not looking. What is wrong with you? Don't you care about me at all?"

2. **Facial Expression Paranoia.** As in, "Why are you looking at me like that? What, is my face hideous and you don't want to say it? You're having second thoughts about this baby, aren't you? You think I'm grotesque and unattractive, don't you? Go ahead and say it. I swear I won't get mad. Don't you care about me at all?"

3. **Our Dwelling Is A Dump-itis.** As in, "We can't bring an infant here. These floors are uneven and the baby can jump out of the windows. When did this couch get so ratty?

There's no tree for a tree house. How on earth is a child supposed to live in this hellhole? Don't you care about me at all?"

And most serious of all . . .

4. **Poverty Hysteria.** As in, "College is going to cost *what* in eighteen years? Did we know that we were so broke before I went off the Pill? Didn't we just have money yesterday? What have you done with it? We'll be raising this baby in a cardboard box under a freeway overpass and that's if we're lucky. Don't you care about me at all?"

All of these symptoms can be clustered under one diagnosis: irritation. Oh, you're not supposed to be irritated at all. You're supposed to spend your days mooning about the house, stroking your swollen belly, and calculating where best to plant the crop of organic veggies you'll need to prepare your own baby food. At least that's the idea you'll get if you're not careful about which pregnancy books and magazines you read. Some of them feature photographs so earnest and groovy that they practically scream, "I make my own yogurt!" This intimidates the Misfit who, though she owns all the equipment necessary to actually cook her own healthy, gourmet food, is now too tired even to deal with takeout.

Seeing images of dreamy earth mothers beaming as they pin a cherubic infant into a cloth diaper makes the Misfit worry, "Am I selfish? Am I unfit? Why am I so irritated by everything right now? Do I even deserve to be pregnant?" If you find yourself asking that last question, you may be suffering from a case of fertility guilt. Fertility guilt is rampant, especially among older Misfits, many of whom go through their pregnancies side by side with friends, colleagues, even siblings who are unable to conceive. Fertility guilt is real, but it's one of those things that no one talks about openly. Do you dare kvetch about your morning retch when you know full well that the woman two cubicles down would give anything to walk in your shoes? And woe to the Misfit Mom-to-be who complains about being fat or out of breath or having to run to the bathroom constantly, only to be reminded how lucky she is to have to cope with such blessings at all. If Misfits weren't such sponges for guilt—some of us have practically made a career out of finding new and increasingly burdensome things to take responsibility for—then we probably wouldn't be so sensitive to innocent remarks that are not intended as criticism. Of course, if we had that figured out, we wouldn't be Misfits, would we?

Emotions run high during pregnancy, and it can be hard to sort out what's real from what's just really hormonal. I occasionally felt obliged to preface a business conversation by saying, "It may only be hormones that make me want to gouge out your eye with this pen, so I'll give you the benefit of the doubt and keep my hands in my pockets till you leave my office." I like to think that colleagues appreciated my levelheaded and forthright acknowledgment of my mercurial pregnant temperament. Or they thought I was psychotic. Either way, no one bothered me with unnecessary meetings. The most important thing for the Misfit Mom-to-be to understand is that she has permission to be sick, fatigued, crabby, weepy, and just plain pregnant. Yours is not the first pregnancy this world will marvel at, nor the last, but it is completely yours and you owe no one any apologies for the way you feel.

Irritation is the natural by-product of the fatigue, discomfort, and hormonal changes of pregnancy. Many pregnant women don't sleep well at night, either because they can't get comfortable, or because they spend so much time padding back and forth to the bathroom.

Getting a good night's rest is a tricky proposition for someone who must get up to empty her bladder three or four times before morning. Don't forget that the baby inside you is a living, moving, rambunctious creature that may well decide to roost either directly on your bladder or worse, on a nerve, possibly causing agonizing lower back pain. Try being a happy camper with no sleep *and* a hot poker jabbing at your spine. And remember that pregnancy runny nose? It doesn't know the difference between lunchtime and the middle of the night, so don't be surprised to be awake, in pain, and flailing for a tissue at 2 A.M.

Pregnant at Work, Radio-Style, Part Two

It sounded good on paper: Fly to an affiliate market, where we enjoyed top ratings and a rabidly loyal following, and broadcast the show in front of a live audience. Beautiful. What could go wrong? After an uneventful flight, we headed out to grab some lunch. The restaurant was selected by our producer, Todd, a man known as much for his earthy appetites as his bleached hair, piercings, and tattoos. He chose the kind of place that offered hot sauce as a vegetable, three kinds of French fries, and two varieties of chicken: fried and even more fried. Seven months pregnant, I gamely dug into a platter of irregularly-shaped crispy things in various shades of brown. Then we headed to our hotel.

Three hours later, I was walloped by a searing bout of heartburn. Ordinarily I have an iron stomach and can eat just about anything, but pregnancy turned me into someone's finicky Aunt Mabel. I needed a Rolaids fix. Bad. Fortunately, our hotel was situated right across a busy highway from a strip shopping center. Unfortunately, the sky was purplish black and streaked by lightning, with rain sheeting down in torrents—a spring storm of near-biblical proportions. Bad as it was outside, my stomach felt even worse. Pulling a bucket hat over my head, I waddled out into the storm.

Is there anything more pitiful than a very pregnant woman in a bucket hat attempting to barrel across a busy road in a downpour? Soaked and harried, I flung myself through the automatic doors of Target and knew for an instant what a near-death experience must be like: It was bliss to walk into the light. I bought a jumbo pack of Rolaids—oh, all right, I admit it—I also got some nail polish, a magazine, and a pack of Twizzlers. It's scientifically impossible to exit a Target without purchasing more than you originally intended. Everyone knows that. Anyway, those Rolaids came in handy the next morning.

We arrived at our broadcast venue, a medium-size concert and sports arena, at five A.M. Everything was in place and working perfectly, which came as a nice surprise. In fact, there was a near-frightening level of efficiency on display. Very unusual for radio. After an hour or so, I motioned Todd over and asked if he knew where the bathrooms were. He led me down a warren of hallways, into a cramped locker room packed with men wearing white uniforms. Todd's explanation that I needed to use the restroom was met with whoops of laughter. "You don't want to be in here! There's a more private one up the hall." The gentleman who offered this kindly bit of advice gestured to his left and off we went.

An hour or so later, the men in white filed into the broadcast area. That's when I noticed that their uniforms were emblazoned across the back with enormous black letters: STATE CORRECTIONS INMATE. "Todd," I hissed. "You brought me to the bathroom with prisoners?"

I learned three things that morning. Number one, radio management will go to any length to avoid paying for help. Number two, when a man says, "Hey little mama, I listen to you every morning in my cell," you'll never forget it. And number three, when a group of guys hasn't seen a woman up close in ages, even a seven-months-pregnant female will elicit the kinds of appreciative glances and low whistles usually reserved for movie stars on the red carpet. It's an unconventional but highly memorable last-trimester ego boost. I recommend it.

Put it all together with the potentially catastrophic levels of anxiety felt by the Misfit Mom-to-be and it's not hard to understand why she might be a little bit edgy. Throw in the bleeding gums, the swollen fingers, and the blotchy face, and then stay the hell out of her way. She's got every right to be irritable—and we haven't even mentioned incontinence.

Kegel exercises are credited with everything from easing childbirth to thermonuclear orgasms. (I'm also told that kegels are the reason that certain professional sex workers are able to pick up quarters or shoot Ping Pong balls with their vaginas. There aren't too many places you'll be able to use this particular tidbit of information, but I'll

---

Pregnancy Lie Number four

Urinary incontinence is normal and temporary. Okay, maybe this is more a hopeful wish than an outright lie. Urinary incontinence is a fancy way of saying that you might pee yourself a little when you laugh, cough, sneeze, or exercise. Any time the phrase *urinary incontinence* comes up, it's generally accompanied by the phrase *Kegel exercise*. The Kegel exercise strengthens the muscles that, among other things, allow you to control the flow of urine. While sitting or driving, simply pretend you're doing just that—contract and release, and then repeat. Most experts advise doing thirty to fifty Kegels per day, though you can do as many as you please with no negative repercussions. The hardest part of a Kegel exercise isn't the squeezing or releasing, it's controlling the expression on your face. Novice Kegelers are likely to purse their lips and wrinkle their brow as they diligently count contractions. While not unsightly or alarming, this sort of grimacing can draw unwanted attention if performed during a staff meeting or business dinner.

Pregnant Play Time!

You should generally start to feel your baby moving in the womb start-ing around week twenty. This varies, though, depending on the baby's position and your anatomy, so don't be a paranoid nutcase if the first day of week twenty dawns and you haven't felt the baby yet. (Note: You will bump into women who felt *their* babies moving at sixteen or seventeen weeks. That's normal too, but these are often the same women who sensed the moment of conception, look great without makeup, and rou-tinely have multiple orgasms, i.e., women who aren't you. These women are to be avoided during pregnancy as they make one feel completely inadequate.) Here's a fun thing to do involving you, your swelling tummy, and a flashlight. Right around week twenty-two, or roughly 150 days into your pregnancy, your baby's optic nerves will have developed to the point that they are responsive to light. Lie down on the bed or sofa, pull up your shirt, and turn the flashlight on. Gently pressing the illumi-nated end against your skin, move the light slowly around. Very often your baby will move in response. It's a hoot! You'll be so excited to be communicating with your baby! Now, don't overdo it and torment the poor tiny thing while it's busy trying to grow and develop. And don't freak out if it doesn't work for you every time. Sometimes the baby is asleep. Sometimes the baby is turned away from the light. Sometimes the baby just doesn't feel like doing what you say—yes, blatant disregard for your parental authority *can* start in the womb.

bet it makes one hell of an icebreaker at a party.) The Misfit who thinks that nothing good can ever be obtained without expending enormous effort will greet the simple Kegel exercise with real skepticism. What-ever her doubts, though, the Misfit *will* Kegel, believing as she does in the virtue of doing everything she possibly can to control every imag-inable outcome. Kegel away—it doesn't hurt, and may very well help.

Not that it worked for me. I'd been Kegeling for years—my interest sparked, I must admit, by numerous articles in *Cosmopolitan* magazine promising the above-mentioned thermonuclear orgasms. With countless Kegels under my belt, so to speak, I figured that urinary incontinence would be the one pregnancy symptom I escaped. Wrong.

On a blustery winter afternoon, having hauled my fertile bulk from treadmill to Nautilus machine at the gym, I stopped by the grocery store to get some juice. Trotting through the parking lot with all the grace and swiftness of a weary sow, I was suddenly overcome by a vicious bout of sneezing. (The pregnancy runny nose!) Mid-sneeze I felt it: that unmistakable warm rush followed by a sudden chill. Yes, right there in a crowded parking lot, wearing nothing but thin running tights and a t-shirt, I peed myself. Mortified, I duck-walked back to my car and collapsed onto the front seat, eyes welling up with tears of embarrassment and self-pity. Huge! Awkward! Incompetent—which, incidentally, rhymes with incontinent—and now afloat in my own urine! Forget feeling capable and confident, never mind glowing and beautiful. What I felt—other than the fabled *not so fresh* of the feminine hygiene ads—was helpless and out of control. Little did I know what excellent preparation that would be for what was yet to come.

6
Ready, Set, Baby!

Just when you're beginning to think you're getting pretty good at this pregnancy business, it will be time to make a dizzying array of important decisions. The first of these will be to figure out just where—and how—you'll be having your baby. Hospitals offer tours of their maternity facilities, along with classes and seminars for expectant parents. Your choice of hospital will be based on a number of factors: geographic convenience; insurance coverage; your obstetrician (your doctor may not have access to every hospital in your community); specialized facilities, like a pediatric intensive care unit; reputation and accreditation.

There are other issues to consider as well. Are you planning what is now considered a traditional birth, one in a hospital labor and delivery suite? Would you like to use a midwife instead of a doctor? Maybe you're contemplating having a water birth. Or a home birth. Or a home water birth using a kiddie pool, a midwife, and an aromatherapist. There are as many ways to welcome your baby into the world as there are parents to dream them up. I admire women who choose to have their babies at home, with candlelight, soft music, and natural healers standing at the ready. Any woman who'll sever an umbilical cord with her teeth is a warrior goddess in my book. But that's not for me. Please, I'm a panicky Misfit. If they'd give it to me, I'd take a Xanax just to watch my dog get groomed. My whole life is constructed on the (so far well documented) belief that Things Go Wrong. I wanted my baby to be born in a hospital.

Keep in mind that hospitals also have a philosophy of care, something that is less tangible than the size of the building or the number of nurses per patient. Of course they all promise to heal the sick and treat the patient as a person and all that blah blah blah. What you're looking for is whether or not their maternity practices are compatible with your desires. For example, many hospitals encourage "rooming in," which is shorthand for the baby stays in your room, not in a nursery down the hall. If that's important to you (it may be, and you'll see why later), then don't be shy about asking about it. And while you're being nosy, also ask about the hospital's C-section rate, access for midwives, and its lactation program. Don't forget to inquire about visiting hours—some hospitals strictly enforce their rules regarding time of day and the number of guests a patient may have at one time. Other hospitals are much more relaxed, especially on the maternity floor, which can be a jolly visitor free-for-all. When you tour a hospital birthing suite, see if it includes a sleeper sofa or a recliner that will convert to a (woefully uncomfortable) bed. That's where your husband will sleep should you wish to have him by your side for every minute of the birth experience. A wily Misfit Mom, I calculated how much melodrama my husband could manufacture out of tossing and turning all night on a hospital chair-bed, and promptly sent him home. I'm going to allow my one glorious maternal moment to be upstaged by a stiff neck? No thanks! However, had something gone wrong I would have wanted him there, and it was comforting to know that we had that option. That's what choosing a hospital is all about: knowing your options.

Childbirth is intense, dramatic, and exhausting. Don't make things more difficult for yourself by having your baby in an environment where you won't get the support you need. This is especially important for first-time moms who wish to breastfeed. The last thing a weary and worried postpartum Misfit needs is a well-meaning nurse or two pressing free formula on her. You'll have your own mother for that. ("Breast-feeding? The baby will starve. I put chocolate milk in your bottle and you lapped it up. Look at you—You Turned Out Just Fine.") Avoid stress later by doing your research now. You'll not only get a wealth of information to help you make your decision, you'll be taking the reins and *doing something*, the thing Misfits are best at. Asking the right questions now will help you feel more in control of the decisions that need to be made later. In other words, stop feeling like a helpless cow and start pulling this project together. We've got a deadline to meet.

While you're figuring out where to have the baby, you must also find a pediatrician to care for your baby. This is a big decision. I know women who put more effort, time, and analysis into choosing their baby's doctor than they did into choosing the baby's father. Crazy, isn't it? But the reality is, you want a pediatrician that you can trust, talk to, and, in a perfect world, rely on to take care of your child until he or she is a teenager. That's an awesome responsibility.

This particular chore kicked my learned helplessness into over-drive. Learned helplessness may sound like an old-fashioned flirting technique involving pretty little you batting her eyes and pretending not to understand how a computer works, but it's much more insidious than that. Children who grow up under extreme conditions of abuse, deprivation, neglect, or terror learn very early that they are powerless in their environment. Adults are unreliable, weak, or, at worst, dangerous. The world is unpredictable, and safety is a shifting and ever-changing uncertainty. These children feel overwhelmed and defeated by their circumstances.

Flash forward to adulthood. The scary people are gone, the child is now all grown up and in control, and the world would appear to be a friendlier and more accommodating place. Yet this now seemingly competent adult responds to even minor challenges or setbacks with a disproportionate level of panic and despair. Translation: The same Misfit who was made to sit in a crawlspace as punishment for being naughty as a child—something she endured stoically and has apparently put behind her—has an utter freak show meltdown twenty years later if the toilet backs up. Why can't she cope? The answer is, in part, learned helplessness. She's been wired to react to any and all stress as though it were a five-alarm blaze that she can never extinguish. Who wouldn't feel strung-out and defeated by that? A good therapist can help you dampen that blaze to an ember, but the Misfit must always be wary of anything that reignites that flame. The funny thing is, it's almost always something small that does it. A Misfit is amazing in a major crisis, and demented in a minor one.

Choosing a pediatrician definitely falls into the minor crisis category, yet it nearly pushed me to the brink. Were there rules? Waiting lists? Protocols? Should I just work my way through the phone book? It took a complete stranger to set me on the right path. I was blundering through a Baby Gap store when she spotted me. Feeling particularly lost and hapless that day, my eyes were tearing up as I stared at a shelf piled high with tiny infant socks. This kindly soul gently took my arm and said, "Honey, do you need help with more than those booties?" After listening to my blurted and snuffling litany of inadequacies, worries, ineptitudes, and general unfitness for my impending motherhood, she offered me a tissue, a hug, and the following advice.

The easiest and best way to find a pediatrician is by talking to other parents. Don't know any? Strike up a conversation with moms and dads at restaurants, shops, and parks. One look at you should be explanation enough as to why you're so interested in baby doctors. Mommies love to share stories and tips, and they're the best resource on the planet when it comes to practical knowledge. Ask enough mothers in your area about pediatricians and you'll soon start hearing the same names over and over. Call those practices and ask questions. Most offer tours and opportunities to meet staff. Finding the right pediatrician is a lot like finding the right therapist: You just feel in your bones that this is someone you can talk to. And that's important, since your baby won't be able to do any of the talking at first. The right pediatrician will trust your instincts, and won't dismiss any of your concerns or worries out of hand. Convenience should be a factor too. Imagine a day in the near future when you'll unexpectedly have to haul a sick infant halfway across town in traffic. This is a journey you don't want to make: when a sick baby isn't issuing a thin, piercing wail, he or she will often be too quiet, gazing at you with a blank, lethargic stare. Either of these states will make you frantic beyond belief. Try to pick a pediatrician close to home or daycare if you possibly can. And make sure you understand your chosen doctor's policies on sick versus well visits. Some practices will not see you without an appointment, period. Likewise, many doc-in-a-box urgent care centers will not treat children under the age of two. That's one more reason why you should figure out your pediatric logistics now, not six months from now at midnight on a Friday or holiday when baby is feverish, vomiting, and screaming inconsolably. Bottom line: talk to other moms, ask them for names and recommendations, then trust your gut. I left Baby Gap that day with socks, a plan, and renewed confidence in my own abilities. Now *that's* productive shopping.

Hospital and pediatrician selected, it's time to attend Childbirth

Badgering the Pediatrician? I Dare You to Top This

Think you're the biggest worrier, the most neurotic nutcase alive? Top this if you can. I had a dream in which my dead grandmother appeared holding a grayish-purple blob in her hand. "This," she intoned, "is neuroblastoma." I woke up in a cold sweat, jumped out of bed, and raced to the computer. Fully expecting my Web search to yield the news that I had some sort of brain tumor—what else could account for my memory lapses, irritability, and frankly, entire personality? To my horror, a neuroblastoma turned out to be an extremely rare form of pediatric cancer, one that generally appears in children under the age of two. I scared my poor husband into whisking seventeen-month-old Olivia off to the pediatrician that very day. Ever the practical Midwestern engineer, Mark could barely choke out the humiliating request to have Olivia examined for something so grave on the basis of a dream had by his crazy wife. But he did it. Olivia's doctor took the request seriously, ordering a chest X ray to be certain. That was a debacle, involving a restraint system that so infuriated the baby that her enraged gyrations rendered the first X rays worthless. Back she went for another try, with my husband grumbling and cursing my superstitious nature, my old-country relatives, and my all-around mental instability. To our endless relief, it *was* just a dream. Olivia was fine. Our pediatrician was wonderful about the whole episode, listening to our concerns and making every effort to ease our worries. It was proof that we'd chosen wisely. Now, she *did* suggest that I get out a bit more and maybe try some lighter reading. She also told me to calm down, relax, and just enjoy my baby. She was right: When it comes to hyper-vigilance, the Misfit Mommy wears out everyone in her path.

Preparation Class. This is what many of us mistakenly refer to as *Lamaze*. Not all prep classes use the Lamaze method. Some are simply highly specialized, detailed versions of high school health class, minus the snickering boys, and with the addition of pillows and snacks. You will do the following in Childbirth Prep Class: Learn to diaper a rigid, plastic, and totally cooperative baby doll; learn the meaning of the

Tell Me He Didn't Really Say That . . .

Put yourself in their shoes: Pregnancy is tough on men. A great deal of what they know about the female reproductive system is the result of one uncomfortable session in tenth grade health class, and a lifetime's exposure to television commercials for feminine hygiene products. Between pitches for satin-smooth tampons (what's the alternative—sandpaper?), various winged things, and douche ads that look like nature documentaries, is it any wonder that they end up a little confused? Our pregnant bodies are fragile and fearsome mysteries to them. Limited to the role of spectator, they don't feel every tiny kick or movement the baby makes. They don't experience the fatigue, the nausea, or the myriad other physical symptoms of pregnancy. Instead, they watch us rapidly morph into moody Humpty Dumptys, with suddenly enormous breasts that are often far too sore to be properly enjoyed. They're every bit as scared as we are of all that can go wrong. They worry about being able to handle their new responsibilities. They feel utterly helpless in the face of our suffering and pain. And occasionally, they say really, really stupid things. Take a look at what some of our listeners have heard from the fathers of their children:

Twins? You're gonna be huge—and you're already pretty big.

You'll be the first woman in history to end up with stretch marks on your face.

I just hope you don't get all ugly like your sister did.

Don't get mad, but your nose is starting to look weird.

Do all pregnant women have so many gross things wrong with them? Or just you?

Damn, woman, even your butt looks pregnant now!

Don't hurt me, big girl!

And my personal favorite, if for no other reason than the sheer folksy originality behind it:

When they're puffy like that, your feet look kind of like pig hooves.

words *transition*, *episiotomy*, and *epidural* (also known as agony, slicing, and blessed relief); watch videos that will be both fascinating and terrifying; and lie on the floor with strangers while your husband or partner is made to give you a soothing massage. How much you enjoy this will depend in part on how social a creature you are. It will also depend on how enthusiastic your partner is. Only the most sensitive and crunchy man will truly relish this aspect of the pregnancy. A really good guy will eventually be agreeable and supportive, but only after you let him whine and complain a little. Don't waste your anger on this. It's perfectly normal good-guy behavior—their patented way of reminding us that they're still men, for crying out loud, and don't want to go watch birth videos with a bunch of strangers.

I understood this a lot better after seeing one of these videos for myself. Most seem to have been shot in the late 1970s or early 1980s and feature earnestly groovy couples who aren't afraid to bare it all.

We watched one that demonstrated the value of using focal objects in natural childbirth to help distract the mother from the pain of a contraction. Pale, sweaty, gasping, and frantic, the woman was at the height of agony when her husband whipped a focal object out of his bag of tricks and implored her to breathe, breathe, breathe. The focal object he selected was a photograph of their cat. Now, some cats have a wise or even wily look about them. Not this one. It was pancake-faced, glassy-eyed, and dopey—hardly the sort of image one would expect to inspire anyone, much less a woman in the throes of childbirth. The whole class erupted in a fit of giggles, and even the instructor was forced to acknowledge that the tape was "maybe a little bit dated." Still, cat and all, you'll walk out of Childbirth Prep Class with a much more realistic idea of what to expect in the delivery room, and that's good. Ignorance fuels fear, and fear robs you of confidence, joy, and sleep.

Not that you'll get much sleep during the last month or so of your pregnancy. You might hear that this insomnia is Nature's way of preparing you to care for an infant who'll soon need you in the middle of the night. Along with tornadoes, hurricanes, and poison ivy, this strikes me as among Nature's dumber ideas. Why not let a pregnant woman rest while she can? But no, you'll be up and down all night, visiting the bathroom, turning from side to side to get comfortable, kicking off blankets, listening to noises, and pondering the Great Misfit Mom-to-be Irrational Questions. These include, but are not limited to, the following:

What if something is wrong with the baby?
Panic over how long it's been since the baby has moved inside you. Take inventory of every drink/cigarette/joint/diet pill/artificial sweetener you've ever consumed and try to calculate odds that are so clearly stacked against you. Despair.

What if the baby hates me?

Likely, considering how much your parents apparently did. Plus, don't all kids hate their mothers nowadays? Fret.

What if I accidentally sit on the baby?

It could happen. Haven't you heard over and over again how sleep deprived new mothers are? This is just the sort of bizarre thing that could only happen to you. Brood.

What if the dog eats my baby?

Who knows what goes on in a dog's mind? Maybe it thinks the baby is a threat. Maybe it thinks the baby is a treat. Don't you remember seeing a movie once where a dingo ate Meryl Streep's baby? That was a true story, wasn't it? Obsess.

What if some lunatic steals my baby from the hospital?

Your baby—wrenched right from your arms! After twenty years of desperate grieving, she returns to you, only to reject you in favor of the kidnapper. Didn't you see a story just like this on the news once? Hyperventilate.

What if I fall down the stairs, drop the baby, then land on it?

You know how clumsy you can be. Add in fatigue, and it's all but guaranteed that you'll take a tumble. Is there time to find a new one-story place to live before the baby is born? Ponder.

What if the baby is allergic to me?

All these environmental pollutants, PCBs, growth hormones in meat—does anyone really understand the effects such things have on a developing fetus? Imagine having to keep your own baby in a clear plastic bubble to protect her from you! Imagine it! Trouble is, you can. Stew.

What if I bring the baby home, change my mind, and want to bring it back?

Aren't babies like bathing suits? No returns, no exchanges? What if you slip and tell a neighbor that you want to return yours and she calls Social Services and they come and arrest you? Ruminate.

What if I die and the baby never knows me and my husband marries some slut who hides all my photographs and pretends that my baby is hers?

Call the cable company immediately and have the Lifetime channel disconnected. And try to get out more—you're going to drive yourself crazy.

When you're not tossing and turning, peeing, gasping for breath, worrying, and trying to convince yourself that having ankles is overrated, and that, despite outweighing your husband, you still look kind of sleek in a Rubenesque sort of way, you'll need to come up with a good answer for all the helpful people who'll be telling you to enjoy your last days of childless freedom. That's kind of like telling a smoker that quitting will extend her life. Yes, she'll say, but it'll extend the *end* of my life when I'm old and miserable and who needs that? Extend my twenties and maybe we can talk. See, "childless freedom" means something a little different to a woman when she's as swollen and dangerous as a peevish walrus. That woman has a giant baby—an actual human being, do you understand?—pressing on her rib cage and choking off her air supply. She's exhausted and her back/feet/legs/head ache. She needs to find a rest room for the dozenth time this afternoon. She's working right up to her due date because really, as she's heard more than once, women in other parts of the world have babies in fields and barely stop hoeing, much less complain, so surely a cushy desk job is no burden for a pregnant woman in this day and age, right?

This is the kind of jovial, moronic chatter you'll hear a lot of in your last weeks of pregnancy. It's best just to chuckle and go about your business. There's no point in getting belligerent; you'll only be viewed with pity and horror—the last things a Misfit wants directed her way. Besides, people usually mean well, and wish only to share your joy. That's also why they want to pat your belly. I know that many women are violently offended by the "pregnant pat" and want no part of having their bellies fondled. I didn't mind, and in fact, was so amazed by the hardness of my tummy that I all but accosted strangers with it. "Get a load of this! It's like a rock! Wait—I think that was a kick!" (Of course, I work in radio and therefore have neither pride nor decorum to drag me down.) For the Misfit Mom-to-be who loathes being touched, the easiest strategy is simply to keep your arms crossed over your body and glower a little. Humans have an instinct for self-preservation that warns us away from any large, menacing, and potentially deadly predator. Become that animal and you'll be left alone. I promise.

There will be times, though, when you'll beg to be touched. Specifically, you'll beg for sex. I know, I know—it seems unthinkable. You're picturing yourself lumbering about the bedroom with all the erotic allure of a female water buffalo and thinking, *not me*. There's no arguing that nine-plus months pregnant isn't exactly the most seductive state of being. Sex is neither easy nor graceful at the end of your pregnancy, even when you do feel like it. Pregnancy may make certain women want to strap on their antlers and go to town, but if you miss out on all that hormonal horniness, don't worry: you'll still beg for sex. Why? Because having sex may help kick-start labor, and if your baby is late, that's all you'll be thinking about. How likely is it that your baby won't arrive on time? Pretty likely. After all, your due date is little more than a very educated guess. Remember all those months ago when your OB asked you for the date of your last period and you were pretty sure, but not absolutely certain? Remember how your OB spun the dial of that little cardboard circle-thing that the pharmaceutical company sales rep gave her? You've hung all your hopes and dreams on a date that was settled upon using that piece of paper and your own spotty memory. And even if that date could be absolutely relied upon, there's still your body and your baby to consider.

Babies are born on their own timetable, not yours. My due date was May 9th—a spring baby! This was excellent news for two reasons: First, I live in the South where summertime heat and humidity can make pregnancy an almost inhumane experience and second, a May 9th birthday would guarantee a Taurus baby, a perfect match for a Misfit Capricorn like me. Sure, we'd both be stubborn, but the Bull and the Goat are famously compatible. With the load of baggage I was hauling into motherhood I knew I'd need all the help I could get. If my baby came late, he or she might wind up a Gemini, and it didn't take more than a cursory glance at an astrology book to know that I was no match for a Gemini baby. Suddenly, my entire being was focused on having my baby on or before May 20. This struck most people as absurd—which is why I tried mightily to keep it to myself. (In a close call, Olivia entered the world at 2:40 A.M. on May 19.)

The tendency to dwell on silly minutiae when so many larger issues are at stake is a beloved Misfit Mom-to-be coping strategy. And surprise—it's a healthy one. After all, who has time to panic over impending labor when there's a Humpty Dumpty wall mural to be painted? Having grown up under battle conditions, we're well versed in the art of focusing on the things we can manage and pushing aside the things we can't. Think of how much you were able to accomplish as a child living in chaos. Things might have been loud, disruptive,

Think You're Tired Now?

It's getting harder to get through the day, isn't it? You're feeling so big and weary, and a little bit foggy and forgetful, too. Even the simplest tasks feel like a burden now. Maybe you're thinking how good it will be to get back to normal once your baby is born—you know, the old energetic and efficient you. Forgive me for laughing, but the old you won't be coming back. Not for about, oh let's see—eighteen years? Kids will wear you out. How many times did you hear your own parents say that? Just wait till you try cooking a big holiday meal with your little precious riding shotgun. Babies adore fire and knives, and are surprisingly adept at snatching them off kitchen counters. Babies also know instinctively the exact perfect moment to produce a colossal diaper or have a shrieking meltdown: twenty seconds before the pot boils over or the oven timer dings. Babies are the reason that frozen fish sticks and delivery pizza exist. I cooked Thanksgiving dinner for twenty with six-month-old Olivia as my sous chef and we barely survived. From her high chair, command central of the Evil Baby Empire, she managed to upend a colander full of green beans onto her head, swat a cup of cranberry juice onto the floor, and bonk the dog on his nose with a wooden spoon. I'll spare you the goriest details, including her wild tantrum mid-baste that resulted in my husband mistakenly thinking that the turkey was finished and ready to come out of the oven. (Food fact: Partially raw turkey cannot ethically be classified as sushi.) *Hectic* doesn't begin to describe it. *Frenzied* comes closer, although *psychotic* is probably the more honest choice. By the end of the day I wanted to drop-kick that turkey like a football, send the Pilgrims back to England, and retire to my bed with a couple of the Valium that the vet gave the cat to keep her from chewing all the fur off her belly. Next year we're having takeout.

even violent at your house, but you still turned your math homework in on time. That's the kind of kid you were—and the kind of adult you still are. The end result of our early training is that Misfits know how to prioritize—even when our priorities don't make sense to those around us. So you want to wipe every surface down with Clorox—go ahead. You want to alphabetize the contents of the refrigerator—have at it. Feel an overwhelming urge to preaddress Christmas cards and it's only June? Do it. Do whatever it takes to help yourself feel competent, together, and in control. Just don't apologize for any of it. We Misfits are forever tripping over ourselves trying to explain or justify our needs and desires. The last days of your first pregnancy are also the last selfish days you'll have for a long, long time. Paint your nails, paint the chairs, paint the town—whatever makes you happy. Enthrone yourself in the living room and demand the kinds of gifts and sacrifices worthy of a goddess as fertile and rotund as yourself. Be high maintenance. Just remember how fickle the calendar can be.

Your due date is just something to aim for, not to get your heart set on. Of course, you will get your heart set on it. Not just because you can't wait to meet your baby, but because you will be so sick and tired of being pregnant by this point that anything, including the alleged terrors of childbirth, seems preferable to dragging yourself through one more long, tiring, humongously pregnant day. That's why the battle cry of the overdue mother is "Get this baby out of me!"

Your next move depends on which bit of folk wisdom makes the most sense to you. I turn to my listeners any time I have a problem, and they have never failed to come up with a truckload of creative solutions. To spur an overdue baby into action, they suggested the following: Eat spicy food (possible entrées range from chicken enchiladas, to Portuguese sausage, to penne arabiatta.) Walk for miles. Drink cod liver oil. Drink castor oil. Dance. I tried them all, and while none of them resulted in my going into labor, I did discover that both cod liver and castor oil are nasty, repulsive liquids. At ten days overdue I was gamely logging three miles per day of walking, eating buckets of salsa, choking down the aforementioned oils, and shaking my oversize booty while watching MTV. Nothing. It was time to bring out the big gun: sex.

"Uh, how, exactly?" was my husband's response to my first invitation to get our late-baby freak on. He had a point. Sex with the nine-months-plus pregnant woman requires limber muscles and a healthy sense of humor. Some women, by the way, claim they never felt sexier than during pregnancy. Maybe you've read about them and wondered why you aren't one of them. Me too. Perhaps feeling sexy during pregnancy, like eating all we want without ever gaining a pound, is something that awaits us in heaven. Both have definitely eluded me here on earth. Anyway, there are solid, biological benefits to prelabor sex.

Nature has thoughtfully packed male semen chock full of prostaglandins. These hormones can help trigger labor by softening or "ripening" the cervix. Nature has also provided the perfect, efficient prostaglandin delivery system: He's napping right now on your couch. Wake him up and say something sexy like, "Babe, give me all your hot monkey prostaglandins." Men love it when we talk dirty, especially when we've got a good fifteen pounds on them and obviously mean business. Taking delivery of those prostaglandins won't be easy, but there are a few options. The first is great news for dog lovers; the second is fun for couples who like to play doctor. Use your imagination, okay? You'll need it to keep from laughing out loud at how silly you're going to look.

This may be the only time in your sex life where you genuinely give no thought to your own pleasure. You may in fact discover a whole new appreciation for the Nike slogan, "Just do it." Really desperate Misfit Moms-to-be have been known to demand two, three, even four doses per day. I badgered my husband so relentlessly that he began looking pale and nervous. "Just let me eat something first," he'd plead.

The Host with the Most

While it's never fun to have a cold, flu, or any other nasty viral infection, it's especially unpleasant when you're pregnant. You don't realize how many great over-the-counter remedies there are to treat a bad cough, a stuffy nose, and the aches and misery of fever until you're not allowed to have any of them. No Nyquil, no Theraflu, no really hallucinatory prescription-only cough syrup. Like the pioneers, the expectant mommy must ride out her illness with little more than rest and fluids to pull her through. It's horrible. Although Tylenol is generally permitted, don't expect that to do anything for your hacking, sneezing, or dripping. Try treating a case of severe bronchitis with little more than decaffeinated tea sometime and you'll never take a twenty-four-hour drugstore for granted again. One doctor who listened to my two-week-old barking cough said, "Well, look on the bright side. You're what? Six months along? Don't worry about the baby. It's a parasite, taking everything it needs in terms of nutrition and antibodies first, leaving you whatever is left. You have to think of yourself as kind of a husk at this point. I'll give you a low dose of amoxicillin. Drink some hot fluids. Stay in bed." For someone who likes to leave a doctor's office with a prescription bearing the warning, "Do not to attempt to operate heavy machinery while taking this medication," being advised to view myself as an ailing husk wasn't exactly the outcome I was hoping for. But as a good host, my options were limited. My little parasite and I took to the couch with a box of tissues, a bag of cough drops, and the TV remote. It's no wonder so many mothers turn themselves into martyrs: We get plenty of practice.

If he faltered at all I'd help him along by barking encouraging things like, "Think of cheerleaders!" This man never dreamed he'd decline sex, but a week or so of romance with a rutting, crabby rhinoceros had him singing a different tune. The poor thing was traumatized. Come to think of it, maybe that's Nature's way of helping him live without sex for six weeks after the baby is born. Isn't Nature amazing?

7

Showtime

The way they carry on, you would think that the baby boomers invented babies right along with laptop computers, mobile phones, and fuel-efficient sedans. While that generation does deserve full credit for all sorts of nifty baby-related gadgets, including monitors, jog strollers, and two-hundred-dollar designer diaper bags, babies have been around for exactly as long as human beings have walked the earth. That's about thirty thousand years. We owe the very survival of our race to the fact that having babies is something we know instinctively how to do. If we had to, we really could give birth in a cave or a field—or their modern equivalent, the backseat of a sport utility vehicle midway between home and hospital. Modern medicine and technology have dramatically reduced the risks of childbirth. Miracles are performed every day in hospital maternity centers, saving lives that even twenty years ago would most likely have been lost. It's easy to think that there are doctors and experts to handle any crisis that might arise. There is one risk, though, that modern medicine can't address, and in fact has helped to create. That is the risk of complacency.

With their bright lights and bustling authority figures, hospitals are
both intimidating and strangely comforting places. Entering one is like
being whisked back into childhood with its plainly stated rules and
incomprehensible reasons for those rules. The message? Someone else
is in charge, so be good, be quiet, and eat your Jell-O. Passivity was
the norm in maternity wards for decades. Women weren't expected—
nor were they encouraged—to be active participants in the birth of
their children. Babies were delivered in operating rooms, while fathers
paced in waiting rooms down the hall. Giving birth was viewed as a
medical procedure, one far too serious and dangerous to permit anything so distracting as a husband, a midwife, or even a mother's opinion. It actually used to be common practice to administer general
anesthesia to laboring women. The poor things would be knocked
unconscious before delivering, only to wake up sore, groggy, and disoriented. No wonder the stork got all the credit.

Thankfully, times have changed. Women are no longer expected to
trade their autonomy for a hospital bed in the maternity ward. Yet so
many of us still do. Even the Misfit Mom-to-be with all of her world-
beating energy, organization, strategy, planning, and control issues,
waddles into the hospital and reverts to a state of abject Victorian helplessness. Why? Because she's afraid. She's afraid of the pain, and she's
afraid of the process. And she's afraid because she doesn't really know
what to expect—and that's because everyone lies about the pain of
childbirth.

Your friends will lie for one of two reasons. Perhaps they arrived at
the hospital, got an immediate epidural, and basically never felt a
thing, leading them to believe that plucking one's eyebrows hurts far
more than having a baby. Or, the second and more likely reason, they
don't want to scare you to death. Unfortunately, those good intentions
can set you up for one hell of an unpleasant surprise when your contractions begin. If you've been told to expect something resembling a

Pregnancy Lie Number five

You will forget the pain of childbirth. No, you won't. You will simply acknowledge that the pain is a fair price to pay for the joy of bringing a new life into the world. That pain is a sobering introduction to a new kind of adulthood, one where the veils of comfort and ease that shield us from the often harsh and naked realities of what it truly means to be human are ripped abruptly away. However, while most such severe physical pain generally yields only greater suffering, the pain of childbirth gives way to joy. That's why the agonies of childbirth so rapidly recede into memory. That's why, if pressed, so many moms look thoughtful and say, "It's really not so bad." Keep in mind too that all human beings experience pain differently. What might seem unendurable suffering for one woman is merely uncomfortable for another. There are women for whom childbirth *is* relatively easy. These are the women who can honestly claim that contractions aren't much worse than severe menstrual cramps. The Misfit Mom-to-be is happy for these lucky sisters, but doesn't expect to join their ranks. After all, nothing in life has come easy for the Misfit; why on earth start now?

severe menstrual cramp, only to find yourself seized by an agony you'd never imagined possible, you're not just going to be scared, you're going to be terrified. It's hard to feel strong and confident when you're in a complete state of panic—and panic has no place in the delivery room.

A fun and useful prelabor Misfit exercise is the creation of a Birth Plan. A Birth Plan is just that: It simply states in writing all of your wishes and preferences for the birth of your child. It's a good way to organize your thoughts and make one last grand gesture of control. It will force you to think about all the steps that lie ahead, and should keep you busy and distracted poring through your pregnancy books and Web sites. Nothing like some last-minute research into epidural anesthesia to take a girl's mind off the fact that in a few weeks an entire human being is slated to enter the world via her vagina.

Once your birth plan is complete, tuck a few copies into your hospital suitcase. Most physicians and nurses are perfectly happy to discuss your ideas with you. My cousin, a turbo-charged Misfit Mom of three and a baby nurse at a busy hospital in New Jersey, hooted with derision when I told her about my Birth Plan. "Please don't tell me you're one of those plan moms! Please tell me you didn't show up with a written plan!" After assuring her that I most definitely had, she explained that most of the moms with plans she'd cared for over the years had promptly thrown their plans out the window shortly after experiencing their first real contraction. Then she broke down and admitted that nurses sometimes enjoy a hearty laugh while reading our carefully designed plans. Fair enough: Babies aren't born according to any plan but their own. The beauty of having a Birth Plan, though, is that it becomes an outlet for anxiety. My Plan was simple:

1. I would prefer that no interns or students attend my birth.
2. I wish to avoid an episiotomy.
3. I want a natural childbirth. No matter how much I beg, do not give me drugs.

There was a lot of other less critical (and apparently hilarious) stuff in there about lighting, music, and my husband being permitted to cut the umbilical cord. It made me happy to think that I was firmly in charge of the entire situation. A limited number of strangers would be permitted to gaze into my birth canal. I'd be allowed to breathe and study focal objects to my heart's content. The lights would be dimmed as my child entered the world. Beautiful. My Plan gave me confidence, which is the best medicine of all. Naturally I chucked the entire thing once the going got rough. But it was a great Plan while it lasted, which in my case was about eighteen hours.

Your labor experience will be unlike anyone else's. Your water may break at home, or it may not. Your baby may come a week early or two weeks late. You might barely reach the hospital in time, or your labor may have to be induced. You may walk, crawl, scream, beg, curse, or howl. You might have your baby in the parking lot, or you might labor for thirty hours straight. Since you can't predict what will happen or how you'll react, it's best to come prepared. Let other, more timid souls shy away from the facts. The Misfit likes—no, *needs*—to be ready for anything. She'd rather freak people out with her detailed grasp of a potentially grisly reality than be freaked out by it. The following are some of the most dramatic childbirth events—and a few of the nastier truths other moms may be hesitant to share:

Your water breaks at home.

Don't worry about confusing your water breaking with one of those laughing-or-sneezing incontinence episodes. Those are just a warm-up. When your water breaks, you'll know it. Expect a sudden rush of warm fluid. Try to maintain your cool and hunt for your mucous plug, which looks just like it sounds. Wrap it in tissue and bring it with you to the hospital to show your doctor. They read those things like tea leaves, so don't be squeamish. Just don't let what happened to one of my listeners happen to you. Her water broke, and in the excitement and panic of the moment she failed to grab her mucous plug away from the cat before he ate it. Now *there's* a treat Purina missed! Yuck. Note: don't expect your doctor to keep a straight face when you burst in with a story like that. Even doctors have their limits.

Your water never breaks.

Movies and novels to the contrary, not every pregnant woman experiences the big splash. Just because you've heard of women having their water break in the checkout line at Target is no reason to assume yours will, too. In the event it doesn't, your doctor may have to break your water once you arrive at the hospital. This is also a minimally invasive method of inducing labor. Your doctor will insert a special tool into your vagina—basically a long, thin rod with a hook at the end—and rupture the amniotic sac. It's painless and quick. Don't squirm—like you haven't had everything but a roadwork crew up there by now? Relax and consider this the least of your worries.

You're a bit overdue and labor just isn't starting.

Your doctor may offer to give nature a push by performing a little service known as *stripping the membranes*. While this sounds official enough, in actuality it's a lot like something you probably did with your first real boyfriend. Your doctor will reach her hand deep inside you, locate your cervix, then paw and scrape at it with the kind of nonchalant zeal that can only be learned at medical school. Be prepared to see stars and dead relatives. This hurts—a lot. If it doesn't, then you should contact Coach immediately and tell them you've discovered a new and sturdier form of leather. Fortunately, your doctor will generally initiate this procedure only when you're past your due date. By that point you'll be so sick of being pregnant that even the prospect of a brisk cervix mauling will be preferable to going another day without a baby. My doctor didn't pull any punches. After she finished up and peeled me off the ceiling, she nodded with satisfaction, and said, "I really roughed you up. That should get things started!" Just brace yourself and don't say you weren't warned.

You're really overdue and your doctor has suggested using Pitocin to induce labor.

You may have heard other women talking about Pitocin and wondered why everyone doesn't use it as soon as their baby is a minute late. Pitocin will start labor, but don't jump to the conclusion that it's necessarily quick or magical. Pitocin, administered via an IV line, will bring on contractions: hard, slamming, painful contractions. The IV line will essentially tie you to your bed, preventing you from walking during the early stages of labor. (You'll see a lot of hall walking in those Childbirth Prep Class videos.) It also means no whirlpool tub for you—a relatively new labor and delivery amenity that can be very soothing, not to mention downright spalike. Why so many restrictions? Because in addition to the Pitocin IV line, you'll be wearing a fetal monitor. This looks a bit like a stretchy belt and is placed around your belly. It's a very simple gadget. However, Pitocin moms are often outfitted instead with an internal fetal monitor. This type of fetal monitor is inserted vaginally (no pain, but a weird twinge) to track the baby's vital signs. (Creepy alert: The monitor, called a fetal scalp electrode, attaches directly to the baby's scalp via a thin wire. It may sound like something out of Frankenstein's lab, but it won't harm the baby.)

Here's the plain truth: Misfit Moms-to-be who plan to have a little Pitocin followed by a soothing epidural just prior to delivering the world's cutest baby may be in for a rude shock. For starters, you don't get to have an epidural any old time you feel like one. Doctors generally withhold epidural anesthesia until the cervix is dilated at least five centimeters. Scenario: You arrive at the hospital dilated one centimeter, then spend hours laboring on Pitocin before dilating enough to qualify for the epidural. Those hours will not be painless, a fact that catches many women who'd been banking on just that by surprise. Pitocin may ultimately be the right option for you, but the wise Misfit uses it understanding that there are no shortcuts and no easy outs when it comes to childbirth.

The epidural gives you the willies.

Let's be honest: It's a needle inserted in your spine. How gruesome is that? It doesn't help that you can't have it until you sign a release form promising not to get mad if anything goes wrong. That it seldom does is slim comfort to the Misfit Mom-to-be who now finds herself with a whole new slew of catastrophes to rehearse. Like hypotension, a dramatic drop in blood pressure that can impact the fetal heart rate. Or a slip of the needle that could cause some cerebrospinal fluid to leak, possibly resulting in headaches that may last for days. Or even respiratory arrest—a temporary, terrifying inability to breathe. Or paralysis. Or seizures. All of which are possible, but improbable and statistically unlikely. Still. The Misfit does like to worry, especially when the focus of her worry is something rare, bizarre, or apocalyptic. It is the Misfit mindset to believe that things that aren't supposed to happen are all but guaranteed to happen right now, right here, to her.

While you're biting your nails over the prospect of having an epidural, it would be wise to find out how your husband or partner reacts to the sight of needles. He'll be right there watching the whole thing, and if he's inclined to scream, faint, or throw up you'll want to prepare for that now. The procedure itself looks fairly simple. You will be sitting up, with your head hunched over your knees. After an injection of local anesthetic to numb the site, you will be required to remain absolutely still while the larger epidural needle is inserted and a catheter is threaded in and taped into place. The anesthesiologist will monitor your progress, administering pain medication as needed via the catheter. What you'll feel is the pinch of that first small needle, then slight pressure as the catheter is inserted. After that you shouldn't feel much of anything, including your own feet. Once the baby is born, the catheter will be quickly and easily removed, and the anesthesia will begin to wear off. Unlike narcotics, which can make you drowsy and disoriented, epidural anesthesia leaves you wide-awake and coherent. Ideally, you'll be pain-free and ready to enjoy your new baby.

The good news about the epidural is that it is widely considered safe and effective. But remember that it's medicine, not magic. Don't expect an epidural to miraculously shield you from all discomfort or pain. This is a baby you're having, not a manicure. View the epidural as a tool, and prepare yourself for the possibility that you might not get to use it. Scenario: With contractions pounding, you career through traffic and arrive at the hospital shrieking for an epidural, only to be told, "Sorry, you're too far along. Time to push." See why you can't count on an epidural to pull you through? When it comes to your pregnant cervix, it's best to think of it as an unreliable boyfriend: It pays no attention to your plans, does as it pleases, and drags you along for the ride.

What if you say—or do—something really embarrassing?

We've all heard the horror stories: the bellowed curses and threats, the many and mortifying bodily functions. Having spent years among amphetamine freaks, petty hoods, assorted scumbags and radio people, I'm pretty familiar with rough language. The fact that I might spout epithets worthy of a pirate during labor never bothered me. There may be countless varieties of Misfit experience, but paint-peeling profanity is generally common to all of them. By the age of sixteen the Misfit is often called more and worse names by her own relatives than many normal people ever learn. Bottom line: So what if you swear in the delivery room? They're just words. Nasty things said

You Say Enema, I Say Enemy

It used to be common practice to administer enemas to laboring women, but many doctors no longer consider it a necessity. Like shaving the pubic hair, routine enemas have largely become a relic of our mothers' time. However, the use of enema as a natural means of stimulating labor contractions has its advocates. The simplest way to find out whether or not your doctor will prescribe an enema is to ask. If the answer is no, and you're extremely anxious about defecating during delivery, you have the option of giving yourself an enema at home. Before you get your doctor's permission and (shudder) drag home an enema bag from the pharmacy, at least give nature a chance. Many women will have loose bowels, even mild diarrhea, in the days leading up to labor. In fact, that's one of the signs to watch for as your due date draws near. Of course, nature may refuse to cooperate in emptying your bowels. If you absolutely must have an enema, do not use a chemical preparation and do not take a laxative. Stick to warm, soapy water and beware: it can be a really unpleasant experience. Afterward, drink plenty of fluids to avoid dehydration. Won't you be glad when all of this is behind you? Ha!

in the heat of labor don't count anyway, so there's no good reason to let a trivial worry like this weigh you down.

Now, there *is* something that no one wants to experience. Something so embarrassing that it's never even joked about. Carol, a publicist and seasoned world traveler who's dealt with more than her share of gross and appalling episodes, put it bluntly: "Fear of defecating on the delivery table has set my baby plans back at least four years." This is the big one, the humiliating, can't-face-the-thought, monster of all minor labor and delivery worries. The phrase "Nurses have seen it all" is a nice sentiment, but the average Misfit does not wish to become part of the "all" that these nurses have allegedly seen. The bad news is, there's no way to absolutely prevent Number Two from happening to you. The good news is, it'll be over and whisked away before you know it. Just make sure that no one is rolling tape to capture the moment. That's one home video you don't need in your collection.

You're terrified of pain—what if you can't handle it?

The simple truth is, you can. And you will. And since you have no way of knowing what to expect, go ahead and prepare for something absolutely mind-bending. That way the only surprise you'll have to deal with is the pleasant one of discovering that having a baby doesn't hurt nearly as much as you feared it would. How well you manage your pain depends on many factors, including duration of labor, your level of fatigue, and frankly, your expectations. Pain *is* scary, and most of us are completely unprepared for the reality of pushing a human being through the birth canal. Men talk a good game about the horrors of kidney stones, but there's nothing like having a human skull banging repeatedly against the inside of your cervix for half a day or so to rewrite your definition of discomfort.

Try to focus on the positives: The pain of childbirth can be very intense, but it is also very brief. There's no such thing as chronic labor, or lifelong labor. It's here, it's gone, you have a baby. That doesn't seem so bad, does it? Plus, our bodies were designed to have babies. Nature wants us to successfully reproduce—that's the whole point. Think of how many wimpy, prissy-girl women you've known who have somehow managed to give birth. These are women who blanch at the sight of a cat choking out a hairball, women who need a Valium to make it through a routine dental visit. If they can have a baby and live to tell the tale, so can you.

Many women are surprised by how strong or brave or capable they feel at the birth of their children. It's not that childbirth somehow grants mothers a mysterious new power. Rather, childbirth is simply an opportunity for women to discover their own often untapped reserves of courage and self-control. The comforts and conveniences of modern life are an effective shield against raw physical suffering, leaving many of us to experience a true trial of our own endurance and inner strength in only one place: the delivery room. In that arena, life is reduced to its harshest, most stark and miraculous terms. It is a place of blood and power and awe, a place where we often meet our warrior self for the first time—and she's amazing. To triumph over ferocious pain is exhilarating. To push your body to its very limits is liberating. And to give birth, an act of creation that is beyond logic or language, is to feel connected to all of humanity. It is an authentic rite of passage, a transformation that forever marks you as a warrior and a mommy.

For the Misfit Mom-to-be, the pain of childbirth is to be respected, but not feared. She has spent her life honing the most important skill needed in the delivery room, the one thing that can't be administered in a pill or from a syringe: faith in herself. The Misfit is a survivor. No matter what you throw at her, she stays upright. She's tough. She's resilient. She has a fairly realistic understanding of How Things Work. Even if all of that is buried under a layer of doubt and insecurity, it's there. Always has been. And now that we've gotten all of the necessary encouragement out of the way, let me be brutally honest and tell you what a real, hard-core, here-comes-a-baby contraction feels like. Ever been shot by an alien death ray?

Natural childbirth is harder than you thought. Are you a weakling?

Let's begin by acknowledging that all childbirth, at least until they figure out how to grow perfect, preppy babies in the J. Crew labs, is natural. Some women choose to go drug- and intervention-free, even to the point of having their babies at home. That's a beautiful, brave, and valid choice—but it's just that: a choice. There's nothing wrong with wanting to have your baby in a hospital, or with wanting epidural anesthesia. Medicine offers many tools to the laboring woman, and opting to use them doesn't make you a sissy. Just know that every choice you make has consequences. There is good research indicating that the more medical interventions you have, the more you'll end up having. They snowball. If that snowball gets big and fast enough, you could find yourself dealing with a cesarean delivery.

Natural childbirth offers some excellent strategies for avoiding medical intervention. Some may work very well for you. I'm a woman who unapologetically loves her comforts and yet I managed thirteen hours of hard contractions by breathing, counting, and hugging a hot water bottle. But when the pain reached a level that completely erased my personality and had me looking for an open window to leap out of, I started asking for help. My husband responded at that point by stepping up his level of coaching and encouragement, gently reminding me that I could do it and offering to rub my back and help me breathe. Breathe? I wanted to rip his eyeballs out and smack him with them. I wanted to club him, the nurse, and then myself with a metal chair. Breathe? I couldn't remember where my face was, much less which part of it ought to be sucking in air. I was sick, disoriented, and insane from pain. Get me an anesthesiologist!

I'd done everything I could to prepare for a natural birth. Unfortunately, my uterus didn't get the memo. Much as I wanted to be All-Natural Heroic Super Mom, it was epidural time. Any doubts I had about a needle to the spine evaporated. They could have come at me with a chain saw if necessary. I'll never regret the hours I spent toughing it out, but likewise, I don't regret the medication. No Misfit Mom needs childbirth regrets or guilt piled onto her load of baggage. And don't worry about the opinions of friends, relatives, or coworkers. Moms don't judge other moms for the choices we make in the delivery room. Remember, we've been there—we *know*.

Your doctor suggests an episiotomy.

An episiotomy is an incision in the perineum, the area of tissue between the bottom of the vagina and the anus. Sexy, I know. Episiotomies used to be commonplace, but are decreasingly so as women have become more active and educated participants in the birth process. Some doctors still perform them routinely—this is one of those things that the Misfit Mom-to-be is required to investigate on her own. Other practitioners believe that it's best to allow the tissues to stretch naturally during the course of labor. (Note: You may hear that massaging this area with olive oil will help prevent it from tearing. I couldn't find any research to confirm that, but who declines a warm olive oil perineal massage? It's like something straight out of *Cosmo*—bring it on!)

Every birth is unique, and sometimes labor progresses so quickly that those tissues rip and tear. That's not only more painful than any episiotomy; it can also have far-reaching, unpleasant consequences. My Misfit friend Marsha is a case in point. Her second child took its sweet time arriving, only to suddenly launch through the birth canal with the force of a missile. Marsha says, "I ripped from stem to stern with that baby and can still feel the damage to this day." I know two other Misfit Moms who tore so badly they had to have reconstructive surgery after childbirth. (Imagine yourself using *this* excuse to get out of a boring meeting: "Sorry, can't. Having my rectum reconstructed that day.") Why doesn't anyone tell you this sort of thing? Because it's horrifying! It's awful! Women would stop reproducing and our species would die out!

Your plan of action: Talk to your doctor, and trust her judgment in this matter. An episiotomy incision is far easier to deal with than a traumatic tear. Why? Because the incision will be nice and even and in exactly the right place. The tear will be jagged and haphazard and much more difficult to repair. If either happens to you, you'll be given narcotics to help manage the pain. You'll also get to experience something very soothing that I like to call a Kotex-sicle. It's a high-tech sanitary napkin that, thanks to some mysterious packet of concealed chemicals, turns icy cold when you give it a good twist. This amazing device—which can be purchased at most home health care stores—delivers a chilly blast of pure relief to the episiotomy site. It's heaven. As for the pain killers, don't be a martyr— go ahead and take the medicine. You won't turn into a pill-popping waste.

What if you have to have a C-section?

A cesarean section is a wonderful procedure, one that may even save your life or the life of your baby. It is also major abdominal surgery. A C-section will add considerably to your recovery time, and it's no picnic to care for a newborn while coping with pain, soreness, and a healing incision. We've come to treat the C-section as a relatively minor complication, which is insane. C-section moms are dealing with all the rigors of pregnancy and birth, plus a full-on operation. As with any surgery, there is also the risk of secondary infection. More rest is required, along with more drugs. It's a big deal—and a procedure not to be undertaken lightly.

Some women, for a variety of reasons, cannot deliver vaginally and must plan a cesarean birth months in advance. These are the seemingly lucky moms who "schedule" their babies and never feel the hint of a contraction. Other women have every intention of delivering vaginally, only to face complications during labor that result in an emergency cesarean. It's tough either way, but the emergency C-section carries extra freight. Why? Because the woman who receives one often enters surgery exhausted and depleted by hours of unproductive labor—hardly an optimal state for such a serious medical procedure.

C-section moms need extra pampering, extra bed rest, and extra support. Fortunately, there are some positives. The scar is fairly minimal, and usually well hidden on the bikini line (though with the current mania for the highly stylized pubic 'do, it's definitely a cosmetic liability). C-section babies are famed for being born with gorgeous, perfectly rounded heads, yielding newborn photos that don't look like outtakes from *Star Trek*. Also, a C-section means no vaginal trauma. As my pal Wendy, a Misfit Mom of two, observed, "At least with a C you can manage your pee. After two vaginal births and Kegeling like mad, I still can't hold it. And it's been *years* since my kids were born."

Wendy's belief that a cesarean delivery prevents incontinence has been conventional wisdom for decades. Unfortunately, researchers have just thrown a bucket of cold water on that notion by announcing that it is pregnancy itself, and not the manner of delivery, that causes women to suffer from urinary incontinence later in life. C-section moms *do* enjoy a brief honeymoon period of a few years, sneezing, coughing, and laughing with confident abandon, before catching up to our vaginal birth sisters in the adult diaper aisle of the supermarket.

If you must have a C-section, take it as the hand you've been dealt. Accept it and be grateful that you live in a time when such wonders are commonplace. Wear your scar with pride and do not indulge any feelings of loss or inadequacy. Fretting over having missed your chance at a "real" vaginal birth is silly and melodramatic. For heaven's sake, girl, after everything you've survived and achieved, you're going to weep and moan over this? Why not look at it this way: You had a baby *and* surgery at the same time! What a woman! As a warrior and a Misfit, we expect you to pull it together. Better? Good. Now take a moment to appreciate what all those junkies are talking about when they say that morphine is amazing. It is. No wonder people get addicted to this stuff. (Note: In about twenty months you'll wish you had a dose when you catch the baby finger painting on the kitchen wall with canned cat food.)

As zero hour approaches, you're likely to feel a nervous mixture of giddy anticipation, dread, and weary impatience. Nature designed the last three weeks of pregnancy to be uncomfortable enough to propel even the most fearful of us to the delivery room. Your bag is packed, the nursery is ready, family and friends are on standby, all anxiously awaiting the big moment. Waddle out for a last night on the town. Take a labor-inducing stroll on those swollen ankles. Seduce your husband into giving up some of those valuable prostaglandins. And ask your experienced mom friends to tell you exactly what having a baby is like. Notice how they can't really meet your eyes; how they pat your hand, their warm and pitying tone as they say, "You'll be just fine."

Getting an accurate, detailed, juicy, childbirth story out of even your best friend is a real challenge. Moms talk about this stuff to each other, but almost never to the uninitiated. Moms understand that it's all worth it in the end, but that can be a tough sell over a glass of merlot to a childless buddy who thinks that a root canal is the greatest physical discomfort she could ever endure. I'll give up the goods on my experience, but remember: Every birth is different, and no one can predict what will happen to you.

My baby was somewhere between five to ten days late (the ever-slippery due date conundrum), I was huge to the point of affecting the tides, sleepless, miserable, and desperate for labor to start. I'd been having contractions on and off, but so sporadically that my body was more shorted-out motor than smoothly functioning baby machine. After days and days, and miles and miles of walking, after a good membrane stripping and more sex than my poor husband ever dreamed of having with a woman who looked like a Tweedle Dum, my doctor decided that it was time to induce.

I arrived at the hospital at six in the morning, and within an hour was hooked up to a Pitocin drip, ready to rock. Contractions began, and they were manageable. I did the breathing, and stared at my focal objects—a pair of tiny red baby slippers shaped like crabs. The hours ticked by, with friends dropping in to visit, nurses offering grape Popsicles, and my doctor periodically checking my progress. That progress was slow, but I was optimistic.

Around five P.M., the contractions began to really intensify. The Scrabble game my husband had suggested as a distraction was shoved to the side. Too bad, because I had a lot of good words to spell: calamitous, searing, gut-wrenching, obliterating, and eye-popping. Everything but the pain seemed blurry and far away. It was spectacular pain, like something beamed in from another dimension. With the contractions only two minutes apart, there wasn't enough time to recover and mentally prepare for the next one before the pain roared back in to flatten me. With my husband squeezing one hand and my nurse the other, I struggled through three more hours, thinking, "Maybe the next contraction will bring the baby." But it didn't, and by eight P.M., I was wiped out, barely coherent, and at the end of my rope.

I hardly remember getting the epidural, though I'll never forget the instant bliss it delivered. Exhausted, I drifted in and out of sleep for the next three hours. At eleven P.M., I still hadn't dilated past five centimeters. After being assured that the baby was fine, I begged for more time. Midnight came and my doctor looked somber. She said, "The baby is fine, but you're not doing so well. You're bleeding, you have a temperature, and you're not making any progress. I want to talk to you about a C-section." I started to cry. I'd so wanted to have natural childbirth, and that hadn't worked out. Now surgery? I pleaded for one more hour. At one A.M., the doctor returned, checked me, and gently gave me the bad news. Instead of dilating, my cervix was actually going the other way and closing down. How perfectly Misfit Mom is that? My cervix took a good long look at what was going on and decided to shut down for business—just my luck. The decision had been made for me. Off we went to the operating room.

A C-section is surgery you'll be wide awake for. The room is both very bright and very cold. You'll be covered with surgical drapes and surrounded by blinking and beeping devices. Nurses will hold your hand and brush the hair from your face. Everyone is cheerful and energized. Expect to hear those five favorite doctor words: You Might Feel Some Pressure. The pressure you'll feel comes from a scalpel making an incision in your lower abdomen, followed by the surgeon's hands reaching into your body, and then pulling out your baby. You won't see any of this, but your husband, costumed like an extra on *E.R.*, will see it all. (Watching the doctor cauterize his wife's veins immediately following her C-section, Steve, husband to Misfit Mom Anne, blurted, "Look at all that smoke!" Not exactly the tender words of reassurance a woman yearns for just moments after experiencing a surgical birth.)

A baby will suddenly appear in the air in front of you, only to be hustled away by a cluster of blue-gowned figures whose faces you cannot read. Then you'll hear a tiny cry, laughter, applause, and shouts of "It's a girl!" or "Listen to those lungs!" Maybe you'll weep too, or throw up your grape Popsicles, and try to croak out, "Is the baby all right?" You might even do all of those things at once. Before you can hold your baby, though, you will be stitched or stapled up, while your baby is cleaned and warmly swaddled. Then it's time for your very first snuggle with your very own baby.

Savor that moment. It's one of the most magical you'll ever know, and once it passes, it's gone, never to be duplicated. You may be weary and shaking or wired and floating as you gaze for the first time into the eyes of this tiny stranger whose heart has been beating in concert with your own for the past nine months. Your baby knows you, your voice, your smell, and wants nothing more than to be cradled close in your arms, held snugly to your breast. Lying with your newborn, there is no pressure to perform, no words to be said, no expectations to be fulfilled. For this little while, this too-brief moment, you can finally rest and allow yourself to simply be. The person you were, the woman who didn't know her own strength and doubted her capacity for love is slipping away now, though it may be a while before you truly believe that she's gone. Try to catch her eye as she leaves, and thank her for taking you this far. Everything you'd dreamed and all that you feared is behind you—and in front of you. You're a mommy for real now. You're a warrior. And this is what it means to be reborn.

From the Department of Pointless Worry

THREE ALARMING THINGS ABOUT NEWBORNS

1) their heavy, wobbly heads
2) their umbilical stumps
3) their soft spot

Which of the above merits genuine terror?

The answer is 2) their umbilical stumps. The wobbly head, while definitely oversize and unsupported by the miniscule and mostly ornamental newborn neck, fits perfectly in the crook of your arm. It takes the average mommy roughly one minute to get the hang of supporting her baby's head. The soft spot, although it conjures nightmarish images of a brain pulsing just beneath the surface of a tender newborn scalp, is a whole lot tougher than it sounds. Gentle handling is required, of course, but the soft spot is not the stuff of science fiction. On the other hand, the umbilical stump *is* serious business. The area must be kept clean and dry both to speed healing and to prevent infection. Immediately after birth, the umbilical cord is cut and clamped. The clamp will be removed before you take the baby home from the hospital. You will then see a dark reddish-brown scab that is often disturbingly in the shape of that clamp. (Misfit Mom Donna brought her baby home with the clamp still attached—a mistake. Two weeks later, when she showed up for her first "well baby" checkup, the nurses stared at her in disbelief. "You mean you didn't know that wasn't supposed to be there?" one gasped. Of course she didn't know—hello? It was her first baby? Make sure that you don't take the clamp home, too. Leaving it on can interfere with healing.) Each day, clean the area very gently with a cotton swab or soft washcloth dipped in warm, soapy water. (Note: Doctors used to advise using alcohol to clean the cord. Not anymore.) Carefully pat dry. Newborn-size disposable diapers are cunningly notched to prevent chafing of the umbilical area, and to allow air to circulate. The scab will fall off within ten days to two weeks, leaving behind a perfectly gorgeous little belly button. Olivia's fell off one afternoon as I lifted her off my lap to make room for a plate holding a turkey sandwich. The scab landed squarely on—you guessed it—my lunch. Which I ate anyway. Who has the energy to be squeamish, much less make another sandwich? Welcome to motherhood.

8

All Yours

Something very strange happens the morning after your baby is born. Sleeping soundly in your hospital bed, you'll be awakened by a stranger's pleasant voice asking, "And how are you this morning, Mom?" You'll crack open bleary eyes and peer around the room, wondering who on earth this poor confused nurse is talking to. Then it will all suddenly come together: She's talking to *you*. *You* are the mom she's referring to. What a scream! Oh sure, you've been called mom before—by the vet. That was all good, tongue-in-cheek fun. This, however, is the real deal. The first time you're sincerely addressed as *mom* is a little bit weird, even embarrassing. It feels kind of like a joke that everyone has agreed to go along with. You know, "Hey, let's call her mom and watch how she reacts!" But that's how it works. Yesterday you were just regular you, and today you are a mommy. It's a brand new identity, one you'll boast for the rest of your life. If it doesn't seem to fit just yet, that's because motherhood is that rare job where you're given the title long before you acquire the skills.

When I heard the inaugural, "Good morning, Mom!" I did two things. First, I threw up the cherry Jell-O I'd just been given for breakfast, then I stared hard at the nurse to see if she was trying to jerk me around. Calling me mom! As though it wasn't perfectly obvious that I was clueless, an idiot, a probable hazard to my own infant. Surely my incompetence was apparent? Should a woman unable to manage even the relatively simple task of digesting Jell-O be permitted to look after a newborn? I didn't know anything about babies and giving birth to one had so far failed to unlock any store of ancestral or evolutionary knowledge hidden deep within me. I figured it was only a matter of time before a social worker was called into the room.

I've come to the (admittedly unscientific) conclusion that there are essentially four kinds of new mothers: the Born Natural, the Guilty Fraud, the Fumbling Worrier, and the Balance Queen. Don't worry about finding yourself locked into a role. You may start out as one kind and gradually become another as your hormones subside and your confidence grows.

The first days and weeks of motherhood are a physical and emotional whirlwind, days where you'll learn more, do more, and feel more than you ever have. It's an enormous challenge for any woman, and doubly so for the Misfit Mom who will second-guess herself on every thought, feeling, and deed. Am I cranky because I'm tired, or cranky because I don't really want this baby? Am I crying because of hormones, or crying because I've ruined my life? Is the frustration I feel a sign of sleeplessness, or a sign that I may be a potential child abuser? Relax, Misfit Mom. Every woman who has ever had a baby has experienced some of the turmoil, mixed emotions, fatigue, and desperation you have. That includes your friends, coworkers, and relatives. Trouble is, by the time you got around to having your baby, their memories of the post-partum period had become dim and pink with sentiment.

That's why it's valuable to have a pregnancy buddy, someone you can speak frankly to about all of the horrible things that tend to get kicked under the nursery rug. New mothers need to share their delivery room battle stories, and like soldiers, seek the company of those who can listen to our tales without judgment. You'll need this now, especially if you don't happen to be a Born Natural or Balance Queen mommy.

The Born Natural

The Born Natural is the star of many a pregnancy book, video, store display, and fantasy. She's the one whose instincts kick in immediately, the woman who takes a single look at her slimy, cone-headed, squalling offspring and falls hopelessly, desperately in love. The Born Natural seems to know just how to hold, feed, burp, diaper, and dress her newborn. She is serene, placid, and moony-eyed with adoration. She feels equipped and ready for the parenting tasks ahead and can't wait to take her baby home. She is as competent and confident as a mother lion.

All of us waddle into the delivery room fully expecting to be Born Naturals. Many of us will be disappointed. Having heard so much about maternal instinct and a love like no other, we're shocked and ashamed if we don't instantly feel those feelings. This is especially tricky for the Misfit Mom, who is already anxious about her fitness as a parent. No matter how together she appears, the Misfit Mom believes in some small, hidden corner of herself that she's damaged goods, incapable of unselfish, unconditional love. Yet at the same time she wants desperately to be a good, loving mommy. Combine lacerating self-doubt and perfectionism with yearning hope, and the stage is set for a very big heartache should the Misfit Mom turn out to be anything other than a Born Natural.

The BN may have an easier time initially, but she's always in danger of becoming insufferably smug. She almost can't help it. Mothering comes so naturally to her, so easily that she is puzzled by and impatient with those of us who don't share her gifts. Born Naturals can get so used to smooth sailing that when childrearing does throw them a curve, they're completely unprepared. In this way they're a lot like the normal people we all know whose idyllic early lives left them virtually unable to cope with even moderate adult hardship.

The Misfit Mom knows firsthand that difficult beginnings have a way of making the rest of the race seem easier. Having to ask for help doesn't make you a bad mother; neither does feeling overwhelmed and underqualified. Never forget that even the Born Natural has to read the instructions before she can operate a Diaper Genie. If you assumed you'd be a Born Natural and aren't, don't despair. You might be amazing with a toddler, a marvel at toilet training. The point is, you can't know all of your strengths this early in the game, and Misfits are all about endurance, not speed. Besides, you're used to doing things the hard way, aren't you?

The Guilty Fraud

The Guilty Fraud is the loneliest new mom, afraid and unable to confess her true feelings. Labor was far more difficult and traumatic than she expected and frankly, she's not convinced it's an experience worth repeating. She wishes people would stop telling her that the pain was worth it, because they weren't there and what the hell do they know? The Guilty Fraud panicked at the sight of her newborn, assuming that something must surely be wrong with its misshapen head and mottled skin. Holding her baby for the first time, she did not feel an all-consuming rush of love and tenderness. She felt tired, awkward, a little disappointed, and guilty, guilty, guilty. Guilt over her lack of gratitude for the child's good health. Guilt over thinking that it looked like an extraterrestrial. Guilt over feeling just a tad resentful toward this howling being that had caused her such discomfort. And guilt, the biggest guilt of all, for not instantly loving this baby that everyone insisted was hers. Guilt! What kind of monster must she be? A bad mother, and a fraud for lying and pretending that everything is wonderful when inside she thinks and feels such ugly, unworthy things.

The Guilty Fraud plays nicely into the Misfit Mom's secret fear that she is good only at acting out the motions of love, not at love itself. The Misfit Mom who wakes up a Guilty Fraud is devastated, but not totally surprised. The shame and emptiness of the Guilty Fraud are familiar emotions for the Misfit and for us, what is familiar feels normal—even when the familiar is anything but. In fact, for some Misfits, feeling bad feels right; it feels like who we truly are. The sorrow of the Guilty Fraud is that she never discovers how many other women have shared her anguish because she doesn't dare admit to anyone what she's thinking or feeling. She pretends that all is well, and struggles to act her way through the day. If she does reach out and confide in someone, only to be berated or dismissed, she's likely to feel more ashamed, more freakish than before.

The Guilty Fraud needs two things: first, to know that she's not alone. Other mothers—good, capable, loving mothers—have felt this way, too. Second, she needs to talk. She needs a supportive confidante, one who can empathize with her struggle. The last thing she needs is a lecture along the lines of "Do you know how lucky you are? Do you know how many women would give anything to be in your place? You should be on your knees that your baby is healthy instead of lying there and feeling sorry for yourself because of a little pain." And so on.

The Guilty Fraud may well be suffering from post-partum depression, a serious illness that until fairly recently went by the mild and innocuous term *baby blues*. Serious attention is now paid to mothers who show signs of post-partum depression. There are a number of treatment options available, including medication for those most severely afflicted. Our mothers weren't so fortunate. Then, baby blues were considered a form of mild hysteria, a bit of attention-getting on the part of the mother that was best not indulged. A woman in her mid fifties recently told me that, after giving birth to a full-term stillborn daughter, she was sent home from the hospital with a parcel of sanitary napkins and the admonishment to "not wallow in useless grief." Her husband was sternly told to avoid any discussion of the pregnancy and the deceased child so as to keep his wife from "getting stirred up." That woman, a victim of an era where depression was only dimly understood, could easily be your mother. Thankfully, it doesn't have to be you.

The Guilty Fraud has permission to feel however she feels. The key is to find someone you can trust enough to speak those feelings aloud to. Silence grants power to even the craziest thought. Sometimes just saying out loud the things that make you feel so evil and unworthy can help to dispel them. Talking can give you perspective. How about your nurse—the one who's seen it all? She's heard it all too, and nurses who take care of new moms can be deeply empathetic and wise. Don't be afraid to talk to her. And when in doubt, remember that Marie Osmond suffered such awful post-partum depression that she fled her family and hid out in a distant motel. If that doesn't sound like a Misfit Mom move, nothing does. If it can happen to Marie Osmond, it can happen to you. In fact, this may be the only thing a Misfit will ever have in common with a member of the super-wholesome Osmond clan.

The Fumbling Worrier

Then there's the Fumbling Worrier. She's so overwhelmed by the experience of childbirth that she hasn't had time to ponder whether or not she's happy about the situation. The favorite phrases of the FW are as follows:

> Is it supposed to look like that?
> Does this seem right to you?
> Is this enough?
> Is this too much?
> Should I do this now?
> Should I wait till later to try that?
>   and
> Do they all have one of those?

The Fumbling Worrier cannot relax. Ever. She spent her pregnancy feverishly wondering if every twitch, cramp, tickle, and nudge was normal or a sign that something might be wrong. Labor was a stressed-out blur of breathing and counting and worrying. Should it hurt this much? Something must be wrong. If she had an epidural, she compensated for her lack of suffering by obsessively watching her contractions play out in big, loopy electronic waves on the bedside monitor. Why aren't they closer together by now? Something must be wrong. Regardless of the fact that she has seen her unborn child numerous times via ultrasound, and therefore knows that the baby is a) human, and b) intact, she fully expected to give birth to some sort of nightmare lizard creature without fingers, toes, or face. She is only marginally reassured by the sight of her own red, slimy newborn, and immediately begins fretting. He's not crying—something must be wrong. He's crying too much—something must be wrong. The Fumbling Worrier needs something to be wrong, because she's convinced that the minute she drops her guard and revels in her good fortune, something really terrible will come along to punish her for being so complacent. It's an endless, exhausting circle and the poor FW can find no rest.

Misfit Moms make excellent Fumbling Worriers. The Misfit has all the necessary skills: resigned acceptance of the unfairness of life; lots of hands-on experience with bad news; and a personal philosophy based on the notion that awful things just keep happening to her. Hardwired for anxiety, the Misfit Mom slides seamlessly into the FW role because at bottom, she just cannot believe that she has a healthy, beautiful baby all her own. Something must be wrong. Well, surprise— something *is* wrong. What's wrong is how much wonderful, fun, joyful bonding time the Fumbling Worrier wastes when she insists on searching for trouble.

No one has ever succeeded in calming an FW down, especially with her first baby. The Fumbling Worrier needs every Misfit resource in her arsenal just to keep from imploding. Research, investigation, list making, stopping crazy thoughts—all of it. It's hard for the Fumbling Worrier to bask in the glow of motherhood when she's so intently focused on making sure that her baby is breathing. And forget feeding the poor thing! The FW is beside herself trying to calculate ounces, time, weight, and regurgitation. The Fumbling Worrier's first days with her infant feel like one long final exam. Question: Does a newborn baby, nursing for fifteen minutes on a train headed toward Chicago, with the train traveling sixty miles per hour, with an average diaper change of twice per hour, need two burps or six? And should his mother be on Paxil?

The Balance Queen

The Balance Queen is the ideal. Not as intimidating as the Born Natural, less panicky than the Fumbling Worrier, more forgiving of herself than the Guilty Fraud, the Balance Queen isn't thrilled to need an ice pack between her legs, but she's delighted to be cradling the baby she's waited so long for. Childbirth was messier and far more painful than she'd imagined, but it's over now. The baby feels good in her arms. She doesn't exactly know how to do everything this tiny creature requires, but right now it seems content to just lie quietly on her chest. The Balance Queen figures that she's handled plenty of challenges in her life, and she'll probably manage this one too. The BQ gives herself time to learn, permission to make mistakes, and the freedom to experiment. She is mindful of the moment, and refuses to let anything keep her from enjoying her first hours as a mother.

If the Balance Queen has a secret, it's this: preparation. The BQ enters the delivery room with a realistic idea of what's to come. She's spent time with an infant or two and knows that taking care of a baby involves a whole lot more than darling little outfits and precious educational toys. The Balance Queen knows that giving birth is one of the biggest physical and emotional challenges of a woman's life. She's not expecting some antiseptic little procedure straight off a sitcom. She understands that a life, a miracle, must be paid for with agony and effort, with her own blood and tears. The Balance Queen is a grown-up woman who comprehends the real truth of having a baby. Maybe that's why so many second-time mommies are Balance Queens.

So there you are, propped up in bed and trying out the name "Mom" for the first time. In bustles a nurse wheeling a trolley with shelves and a little boxed-in mat on top. Lying on the mat is your tightly swaddled newborn, all pink, squishy face and sleek, downy hair. Your heart skips a beat. You reach out to take the baby, but no, it seems the baby is going to be needed for a little demonstration first. The baby nurse compares your paper bracelet to the baby's—hospitals are very identity- and security-conscious now. Once she's established that everyone is in the right room, it's time for a diaper and swaddling lesson. Everything you need is on the trolley: wipes, tiny newborn diapers, extra blankets. Diapering a newborn is pretty simple since the baby really can't put up a fight. That's helpful for first-timers who are all thumbs and don't yet know that any kind of lotion or moisture will render the adhesive on the diaper tabs completely useless. Once the diaper is off, you must clean the area, but quickly so the baby doesn't get chilled. Newborn skin is so delicate that you'll most likely wipe with just a soft cloth moistened with water—anything else would be unnecessarily harsh.

Next, you'll get to use that mountain of thin, cotton receiving blankets that piled up at your baby shower. Hospitals have apparently banded together and agreed that their receiving blankets must all resemble the dishcloths your great-grandma had hanging in her kitchen, but they are the perfect size and weight for wrapping an infant. Swaddling involves placing the baby in the center of a blanket, then wrapping his or her extremities close to the body for warmth and security. Newborns feel comforted and safe when snugly wrapped. Think of swaddling as a womb substitute. There's an art to it. A properly swaddled baby looks a bit like a burrito. Be prepared to struggle mightily with this. Your baby nurse can perform a professional swaddle in about twenty seconds with only one hand. You, however, will use both hands and a knee and take three to five minutes to create a sloppy wad with an irritated and impatient baby poking out of it. (Note: Your husband will instantly display a level of swaddling dexterity that will drive you mad.)

Once you've convinced the baby nurse that you can change a diaper and do a reasonable swaddle, she'll prepare to leave the room. She'll tell you exactly how to reach the nursery if you have a problem, and she'll tell you when your baby is due back for a checkup or a headcount, or whatever it is that's done to babies in hospital nurseries. Wait, you'll say. I'm allowed to keep the baby with me for as long as I want? The baby nurse has heard this before, and will respond by pointing out that it is, after all, your baby. She'll tell you that some mothers keep their babies with them around the clock, a practice known as *rooming in*. She'll also tell you that some mothers would rather sleep while they can, and choose to leave their babies in the nursery. It's up to you. At that point she'll march out of the room, leaving you completely alone with your baby. How crazy is that?

These next few minutes are critical, so pay attention. You will most likely be besieged with well-meaning visitors who want to coo over the baby while giving you a token nod. Time alone with your newborn is brief and precious and you are entitled to take advantage of every second of it. Try to see through your baby's eyes. For over nine months she's been in a dark, warm, safe place. Everything was provided, everything made sense. Then suddenly, bright lights, cold air, the too-loud voices of strangers, fingers poking and prodding her, and where did mommy go? Can you imagine how lost and afraid she must feel?

Scoop that baby up and pull her close. You have been her entire universe. After living inside your body next to your heart, she misses the sound and smell and rhythm of you. What she craves is to be next to your skin, so pull that blanket off, put her right on your bare chest, then snuggle up warm and close. For the Misfit Mom who always wants to be sure she's doing the right things, research shows that skin-to-skin contact helps babies regulate their temperature, heartbeat, and respiration. Do this, even if you're tired, crabby, or just plain don't feel like it. Do it because this is another of those moments that slips away, and there's no rewinding for another chance. Do this as much for yourself as for your baby. The smell and feel and weight of your newborn child against your own skin helps to dissolve the knot of fatigue, soreness, and self-doubt that so many of us feel after giving birth. Some women will be uncomfortable with skin-to-skin contact, but the Misfit shouldn't be one of them. After all the freakiness you've seen, you're going to be weird about your own body or that of your child? When you hold your baby skin-to-skin you're merely responding to an instinctive directive. This comes as a shock to those women who apparently believed that the maternal instinct had more to do with making the right choice between Minute Maid and Juicy Juice. Parenting has become such an enormous commercial enterprise that it's easy to get instinct confused with marketing propaganda.

Despite our best efforts to pretend otherwise, we are animals, and it's in our best interest to successfully reproduce and rear our young. The knowledge required to raise them is encoded in our genes. Yes, we've improved on the wisdom of our ancestors in all sorts of ways. But they weren't entirely stupid or we wouldn't be here to roll our eyes at their primitive methods. The most Misfit Mom is chock full of maternal instincts—even if she doesn't think so. We took calls one morning on the show from listeners who had gone to extremes for a pet. One woman described prechewing chicken so that her elderly shih tzu could gum it down. I told her, "You're gonna make a great mom one of these days!" She replied, "Oh, no. I don't have any maternal instincts." Please! We all have them, but if you're prechewing your dog's dinner, you've got them to spare.

Instinct is a compulsion, a voice that whispers urgently, "This is the way." Trust that voice, and not your shrieking sister-in-law who wants you to take your infant off your chest immediately and muffle it up in a scratchy and hideous knitted shawl. Trust yourself and believe that all you need to do is be present, to touch, and cuddle. That's it. Your baby has no desire for a designer romper, a teddy bear, or a rattle. All your baby wants is you, and to be as close to you as she can possibly get. What could be easier than that?

Feeding sure won't be. Not because feeding a baby is hard, but because no matter how you do it, there will be a deafening chorus of opinions to the contrary. You might as well resign yourself to having your ears chewed completely raw, because the last woman who fed her baby in absolute peace probably lived in a covered wagon. The invention of commercial baby formula ushered in the intense and often ugly debate of bottle versus breast.

Full disclosure time: I'm a passionate breast-feeding advocate. I didn't plan to be. It took me by surprise, if you want to know the truth. I always thought of breast-feeding as a good thing, and as something I'd like to try, but I was never a lactation loony. Now I kind of am, a little bit. But please don't run away. I've had a lot of women approach me in places ranging from the hair salon to the drugstore to tell me that they weren't going to breast-feed, but after hearing me talk (and joke) so positively about nursing on the radio, they gave it a try—and it was the best decision they ever made. That makes me want to spread the word even further. Nursing is good for both mommies and babies, but if it's not your choice or doesn't work out for you, relax. Misfit Moms never judge, second-guess, or criticize each other's choices. We're too busy judging, second-guessing, and criticizing our own.

The Misfit Mom approaches the question of how to feed her baby the same way she approaches everything else: by trying to make the decision that will positively impact and please the greatest number of people. The Misfit Mom wants to do as much good as she possibly can.

She also has a chip on her shoulder, one that digs and jabs and slyly asks, "Are you a good enough mother?" That's why feeding can be a serious issue for Misfit Moms.

Unless you've been hiding out in the woods for the past decade, you probably know that breast milk is considered the optimal food for human babies. Formula manufacturers know it too, which is why they're at such pains to unlock the mysteries of human milk so that they can duplicate it in their laboratories and become even more insanely rich. When scientists recently announced that certain compounds in breast milk aided in neurological development, formula manufacturers rushed a new product to the shelves boasting some of those same compounds. But breast milk is a wily thing, tricky to pin down under a microscope. For starters, it changes all the time to meet the varying needs of your developing baby. Formula can't do that. Breast milk provides your infant with all sorts of helpful antibodies; formula doesn't. Breast-fed babies suffer fewer ear and gastrointestinal infections. Researchers are now saying that breast-fed children have higher IQs and lower rates of obesity, along with lower rates of some childhood cancers. Breast is best, but not everyone can or will nurse.

Before you panic and berate yourself for giving your baby formula, remember that most of us were bottle-fed and we turned out fine. There are brilliant thinkers, gifted artists, and all-around good people who sucked down nothing but formula as infants. Likewise, I'll bet there are more than a few cold-blooded psychos rotting away in Supermax prisons who were fed only breast milk. How you feed your baby will not make him or her a genius or a criminal. It can, however, make *your* life easier or more difficult. Know that how you feed your baby will affect your whole family, so whatever you choose, make sure that you and your husband or partner are in agreement. Whether you breast or bottle feed, his support is critical. Let's break it down:

BREAST MILK	FORMULA
Free	Expensive
Readily available, self-renewing	Sold at grocery stores
Always the right temperature	Must be carefully heated
Self-dispensing	Requires clean, sterilized bottles, nipples
Customized for your baby	A few different formulations available
Less malodorous diapers	Diapers reek to high heaven
Easily digested	Can cause constipation
	Allows for other caregivers to easily feed the baby and saves Mom the effort of pumping

It may look like I'm stacking the deck in favor of nursing, but the facts stand. While there are no guarantees, breast-fed babies are generally healthier. A healthy baby is a happy baby, and a healthy, happy baby is easier to care for. That makes a mommy's life easier, too—and there's nothing wrong with that. Breast-feeding is a fairly simple thing, but it does take a bit of practice. It involves some basic technique and a little bit of knowledge. It's not supposed to hurt, and if the baby is latched on correctly, it won't.

Hospitals have lactation consultants on staff who are eager to help new mothers master the art of nursing. Not surprisingly, many women are freaked out by the prospect of a complete stranger manhandling their boobs. Americans are fixated on breasts in every aspect but the one that nature intended them for—isn't that funny? Anyway, a proper latch is the secret to successful breast-feeding. Lock that baby on and the rest takes care of itself. A proper latch, incidentally, does *not* consist of the baby gnawing, jawing, chewing, or mauling your nipple. Instead, the nipple will actually be in the back of the child's mouth, with the baby exerting pressure on the aureole. This is why it's important that your baby open his or her mouth wide as you bring your breast in for a landing. Although your infant will have both instinct and appetite for nursing, your help is needed to make sure that everything goes well. Try not to get frustrated! Neither of you has ever nursed before—and one of you is just a few hours old, for pity's sake.

Milk flow and quantity are big issues for nursing moms, because our breasts don't come conveniently marked with available ounces—it's the one tattoo I haven't seen, come to think of it. Then there is the potential discomfort of having too-full breasts, a sensation that can range from warm and tingling to a painful burning and throbbing. The act of nursing regulates milk production naturally, and regular nursing should eliminate the problem of engorgement. Who hasn't heard horror stories about that? Breasts as hard as rocks, accompanied by searing pain . . . no thanks, right? It really can be avoided. Allowing your baby to nurse on demand for the first few weeks will get your nursing off to a good start. Demand nursing, which follows the baby's hunger cues (rooting, mewling, attempting to suck, crying), not some ideal schedule that you or a well-meaning family member had in mind, will drive many people you know completely insane. You will be hectored relentlessly on the subject of how the baby is manipulating or training you. You'll be told that the baby is using you as a pacifier, or nursing simply for comfort. (News flash! You're his mommy—where else should he turn for comfort? A hit of Chivas and a hooker?) Newborn babies are incapable of practicing psychological warfare. They nurse not to terrorize you, but simply because they need to eat, and they crave close physical contact with mommy. A demand-nursed newborn will eventually (and naturally) assume a more regular and less frequent feeding schedule.

It *is* true that breast-fed babies eat more frequently. That's because breast milk is more easily digested than formula, and clears the baby's system more rapidly. That's exactly what's supposed to happen. Trying to stuff a baby full of food in hopes of making it sleep is a wishfully nutty plan, more often resulting in a baby with painful gas than a little Rip Van Winkle. Just because our mothers crammed everything from rice cereal to Quaker Oats into our bottles to fill us up and knock us out doesn't mean it's smart to follow in their footsteps. If newborn humans could eat like bears and hibernate like them too, nature would have designed us that way. Human babies require frequent feeding, changing, and holding. They're helpless and utterly dependent, and when they yip and squall it's not to torture you but rather, to make sure you don't wander off and forget them underneath a bush.

There is one little detail about lactation that you should know, and it's something that may happen to you no matter what your feeding plans are. Your body will fire up the engines of lactation even if you have no intention whatsoever of nursing. Those engines will eventually shut down if you don't nurse, but every new mother has to live through the start-up. Breast milk doesn't begin flowing immediately. The first fluid produced is a nutrient-rich powerhouse of a substance called *colostrum*. Colostrum offers your newborn so many benefits that even nursing for only a few days gives your baby a real health advantage.

Your actual milk will take a few days to come in. When it does, you may experience something that back in the old days used to be called a milk fever. Milk fever feels just like it sounds. You'll run a temperature and feel achy and unwell. The unwitting Misfit Mom who wakes with a fever in the middle of the night three days after giving birth is likely to have one thought: infection. Her mind will then race with the imminent possibilities of a tragic, untimely death, and a motherless infant. It will take a frantic wee hours phone call to the obstetrician to confirm what your great-grandmother could easily have told you: Your milk is coming in. No one will warn you about milk fever because a) they don't know it exists, or b) they forgot. Unfortunately, neither ignorance nor amnesia can provide any comfort to the feverish Misfit Mom at two in the morning. The good news is, milk fever doesn't last more than a few hours. The even better news is, now you know what to expect. And speaking of expectations, let's take a look at some of the expectations and questions surrounding nursing—including some that you may be hesitant to speak out loud.

Breast-feeding is "dirty." It creeps me out.

Americans are a little bizarre sometimes. We suffer from a gigantic, cultural boob fetish, and yet we squirm in embarrassment when a mother suckles her baby. Hate to be a buzz kill, but nursing is what breasts are for. Sure, they're useful for lots of other neat stuff, too, but let's not forget the real reason we have them. The only things perverted or sick about breast-feeding are the sick perverts who consider it a sexual activity and get off on it. Surf the Internet if you don't believe me.

Nursing will destroy my breasts.

"Destroy" is kind of a harsh word, one that ought to be reserved for things like fire and the atomic bomb. The average woman experiences a substantial increase in breast size as a result of pregnancy. When your breasts return to their pre-pregnancy dimensions, you may notice a bit less elasticity and a bit more sag. That's natural. Women who never nurse a day experience that, too. I nursed for thirteen months and I'll tell you, I think mine look pretty good. But every woman's body is different. It ultimately comes down to priorities. How much topless dancing were you planning to do after your baby is born? Does having a great rack outweigh the benefits of giving your baby your milk?

But if I nurse I'll never get any rest or a break.

Not true. Breast milk can be pumped and stored in the freezer or refrigerator. That way your loving partner and family members can bond with baby in the middle of the night, and while you're off getting your highlights done.

Nursing means having a baby glued to your body 24-7 and I can't handle that.

Well, you were aware that human babies were helpless, dependent little creatures, right? If you did your homework, you know the difference between getting, say, a cat, and having a baby. You chose a baby because you wanted to be a mommy. Being a mommy means being available. Misfit Moms learned that the hard way through the heartbreaking absence of their own mommies. Nursing does force you to be absolutely present for your child at feeding time. There's no propping your breast in the crib and going off to check your e-mail. Nursing mothers spend a great deal of quiet time with their babies, and that's a wonderful thing for *both* of you. Are you so busy and important that you can't halt the whirlwind long enough to feed your infant?

If I'm breast-feeding, how will I be able to tell how much the baby is eating?

Here's a booby trap (sorry—couldn't resist) just waiting to claim the Misfit Mom. She needs to be so absolutely certain of things. Trust that your baby will eat what he needs. They're not like us—starving ourselves here, gorging there. They eat to satisfy hunger. An obsession with ounces is fine as obsessions go, and even necessary under some circumstances, but it shouldn't overtake your life. Nursed babies can take in more volume more quickly than bottle babies, and you might get a voracious little chowhound who gobbles a meal and moves on. Or you might have a little dreamer who likes to sip slowly while gazing in rapt adoration at your face. As time goes by, you'll get to know your baby's eating style and schedule and if you let him nurse when he's hungry, he'll be well fed. Believe me: After a while you'll be a total expert on the subject of your baby. You'll *just know*. Those tricky maternal instincts again. Also, a hungry baby is a loud baby—they tend not to suffer in silence.

Pumping is gross and creepy and I just know I won't be able to do it.

First of all, no it isn't. And if it is, it's certainly no more gross or creepy than any number of other things we do every day, including certain sexual acts that you've been known to enjoy on occasion. If you're determined to pump, you can and will. I pumped every weekday for nine months while sitting on the floor of my office during a two-song break that we scheduled each morning in our show. If I can pump six ounces in under ten minutes while listening to the Goo Goo Dolls for the thousandth time, then *any* woman can pump. We talked to a military mom on the air right after she'd returned from deployment in the Middle East. While stationed in the desert, she pumped milk four times a day, every day, then poured it down the drain just to keep her milk flowing so she could resume nursing her baby daughter when she finally got home. Now that's a warrior mommy—America's enemies don't stand a chance against that kind of determination.

What happens when you're totally committed to nursing, only to discover that you can't?

If you're a Misfit Mom, your first impulse is to pull out your hair and wallow in grief and self-recrimination. Please don't. Nursing doesn't work out for everyone, for a variety of reasons. Some babies can't suck effectively. Some mommies have problems with their nipples. Health considerations may be a factor. The point is, you did your best—and that's all any mommy can do. As women, we are so quick to condemn and loathe ourselves for every perceived inadequacy. Don't let feeding your baby, which should be a joy and a pleasure no matter what method you use, become yet another suitcase that you stuff full of guilt. That's wasted energy. Relish every minute that your baby gazes into your eyes while eating and know that you're doing a great job. If you need extra bolstering, remember that your mom put Tang in your bottle—and it didn't stop you from growing up to be smart and adorable. I even know one brilliant woman with degrees in both business and law who was routinely given Mountain Dew in her baby bottle. I know, I know—our parents had less sense than monkeys.

Now you've got some of the basic mommy skills covered. You're diapering, swaddling, feeding, burping, and holding the baby without worrying too much about whether or not you're doing it right. Everything's going pretty smoothly, and you're anxious to get home to your own bed, your dog, and the circus animal nursery you spent so many hours decorating. You're starting to get used to being called "mom" even if you don't yet feel one hundred percent worthy of the title. Then something will happen, something that helps you understand just how much a mommy you've become. As Misfit Mom Teresa put it, "I was in my hospital room when I heard faint crying coming from down the hall. Suddenly, the hair on the back of my neck stood up because I knew: That was *my* baby crying. She was only a day old but somehow I knew her cry. I was up and out the door of my room and halfway down the hall toward the sound before I even realized I'd moved. That was the first moment I really felt like someone's mommy."

While many mothers feel intensely protective and possessive of their newborns, these feelings are a revelation for the Misfit Mom. Couple that with her ability to identify her baby's cry, or the discovery that her touch has the power to soothe and comfort her child, and the Misfit sees joyful signs that she just might turn out to be a decent mommy after all.

Elated by this heady discovery, the Misfit Mom is bundled into a

---

All Hail Her Majesty, the DQ

When you're down in the diaper trenches, it's easy to lose sight of just how different things really are once you have a baby. Sometimes it takes a collision with your former self to realize how very far you've come. When Olivia was about four months old, my husband and I took her to Charleston, South Carolina, for a long weekend. One evening after dinner we took a walk, pushing Olivia in her stroller. The street was crowded with tourists and students. Traffic was bumper-to-bumper. An SUV full of beautiful college girls pulled up alongside us. The windows were down, and the stereo was blaring. All six of the girls were singing along to Abba's "Dancing Queen." They were tan and gleaming and probably had no idea that they were experiencing one of the most carefree moments of their young lives. I was riveted. Then the light ahead turned green, and the girls drove off, the sound of Abba growing fainter and fainter until it was gone. Gazing at Olivia, all plump and pink-cheeked in her nest of blankets and squeeze toys, I started to laugh. I used to be the dancing queen. Now I'm the dairy queen. Still royalty— it's great to be a mommy!

wheelchair for the ceremonial journey to the hospital's front door. All of the past nine months, every anxious hour, has been leading up to this moment. You're about to be turned loose with your baby, shoved into the wide world to fend for yourselves. As the elevator descends and you draw ever closer to freedom, the reality begins to dawn on you. They're just going to let you stroll out of here with this baby, no questions asked. In moments, you'll strap this helpless being into a car seat and head for home, where every decision, every choice, every mistake is yours to make. Rolling through the lobby clutching your baby, you bask in the delighted smiles of passersby, all of who light up at the sight of your beautiful new family. Outwardly, you're the very picture of beatific maternal calm. Inside though, you're frantically taking inventory of all the things you still don't know. That list seems to have gotten a whole lot longer since the last time you checked. Then you're outside, squinting a little in the bright daylight. Ready or not, you stand up and, with your baby, take your first step into your brand-new life.

9

WHAT Time Is It?

When pregnant women try to envision themselves at home with an actual baby, a lot of hazy, soft-focus pictures swim into view: trips to the park, playful bubble baths, long, quiet lunches with friends, baby snoozing peacefully in a carrier at your side. Very few of us picture ourselves wearing flannel pajama bottoms, a faded "Too Drunk to Think" t-shirt, flip-flops, spit-up, and a glazed look. Which do you think is closer to reality? If you had the good sense to pick "Too Drunk to Think," congratulations! Realistic expectations are a new mommy's best strategy.

Babies are hard work. Like most first-time mommies, I didn't understand how that could be until I had one. They're cunning, these babies, the way they lull you into thinking that they're harmless, immobile beings that spend most of the day sleeping. That's a big old dirty lie. Sure, they sleep a lot—some of them. Some babies don't, and a wakeful baby will put you through mental and physical maneuvers that the Marines would consider unduly harsh. A baby can be a brutal, time-sucking taskmaster. Talk about the toughest job you'll ever love! Let's take a look at a typical newborn/mommy day:

4:40 A.M. Please, God, please do not let that be Baby crying. Pretend not to hear; maybe husband will handle it? Husband handles it by handing Baby over to you to be nursed. Husband tells you how wiped out he feels. Listen to him snore while feeling sorry for self. Drift off to sleep as Baby nurses.

7:15 A.M. Baby mewling; hungry again? Unable to open own eyes— have they been glued shut in the night? Cuddle Baby close and babble soothing nonsense like, "Let's go back to sleep." And, "Mommy will give you a thousand dollars if you please go back to sleep." Baby's much too clever to fall for it—a sign of budding genius? Drag yourself to your feet. Change diaper.

8:00 A.M. Install Baby, looking extremely precious in fuzzy yellow bunny pajamas, into battery-operated swing. Wonder briefly how the pioneers managed without it. Hunt through kitchen for tea bag. Fail to find one. Glance at Baby just in time to see arc of vomit shooting toward kitchen floor. Rush to swing, scoop up Baby, and call dog over to clean up mess. Stub toe on baseboard, curse, apologize, rush baby to changing table for clean-up.

8:20 A.M. Return to kitchen. Reinstall Baby, now looking adorable in cheetah print leggings and matching cap, in swing. Stare blankly at dog, still licking the floor in front of the swing. Ponder the "dog's mouth is cleaner than a human's" conundrum and calculate whether or not dog saliva is equal to Mr. Clean. Resolve to mop later. Eat piece of peanut butter toast standing up next to sink. Answer ringing phone with mouth full of peanut butter. Mumble incoherently at telemarketer and hang up. Why is Baby crying?

9:00 A.M. Baby is asleep! Time to shower, blow dry hair, throw clothes into washer, put away dishes, read newspaper, return phone calls, walk dog, and spend quality time with husband. Do none of those things. Instead, fall asleep on couch watching *Changing Rooms* on BBC America. Drool.

10:45 A.M. Wake with a start. Creep in to bedroom and spy on baby. Still sleeping! Race to bathroom and turn on shower. Lather hair, put head under spray; hear Baby scream. Frantically rinse out shampoo while scrubbing furiously at self with soap. Baby is howling. Run out of shower soaking wet and grab Baby out of bassinet. Baby is immediately silent. Wade back into bathroom. See dog lapping water from floor. Good dog.

11:30 A.M. Nestle Baby, fed, content, and looking stylish in a cream-colored sleeping gown, into carrier on floor. Dump clean laundry out of basket, sit down and begin folding. Show Baby a sock. Show Baby a t-shirt. Show Baby a hand towel. Put hand towel over your face, then yank it back while singing, "Peek a boo!" Gaze adoringly at Baby's perfectly round head and silky hair. Stare at Baby. Baby is gorgeous.

12:00 P.M. Attempt to wear Baby in sling. Step One: Struggle to make sense of baffling instructions. Step Two: Struggle to cinch sling over shoulder. Step Three: struggle to stuff uncomprehending Baby into sling. Step Four: Shuffle gingerly toward refrigerator. Try not to bump Baby's head on door. Eat slice of cold pizza standing up next to the sink. Change diaper.

1:00 P.M. Time for a walk. Ease Baby out of sling and back into carrier. Remind self that Baby is not yet capable of giving you a skeptical look. Find shoes. Call dog. Find leash. Find sunglasses. Find mobile phone in case of emergency while walking. Go to the bathroom. Snap carrier into stroller. Holding dog with one hand, attempt to push stroller. Fiddle with sunshade. Dog wants to run. Yell at dog. Yell at dog again. Return dog to house. Resume walk. Observe how sunlight illuminates milk and pizza grease smears on your shirt. Sigh. Point out landmarks to Baby: "Look! The Fed Ex man!" Hope for neighbors to come out and admire Baby. Watch Baby's eyelids flutter. Baby is asleep.

2:00 P.M. Carefully ease sleeping baby into crib. Write five thank-you notes. Unload dishwasher. Return three phone calls, every one of which begins with a cheery, "How's the new mom?" and ends with a solicitous, "Call me if you need anything!" Wonder darkly if "anything" includes popping by around two in the morning for a little diaper-and-burping time. Stand next to sink and guzzle glass of water. Stare blankly into space. Realize you have not yet brushed teeth.

4:00 P.M. Baby awake and howling to eat. Change diaper. Settle into chair and nurse Baby. Read magazine while Baby nurses. Think: This isn't so hard. I can do this. Feel contentment. Burp Baby. Bounce Baby on knee. Say, "Who's a bouncy-wouncy bear? Who's a teeny-tiny kitty?" See Baby spew a mighty fountain of barf. Feel the warm liquid sink into your pants. Does Baby feel much better now? Clutching Baby with one hand and barf-soaked lap in other, hobble into bedroom. Change pants. Change diaper. Change Baby's outfit.

5:00 P.M. Pretend not to hear husband exclaiming over quantity of laundry in basket. Let machine pick up ringing phone. Lie on couch. Prop Baby on lap. Study Baby. Baby, looking downright jaunty in striped teddy bear coverall, stares back. Baby is shockingly cute. Understand sappy love songs on radio for first time. You are my everything. The power of love. The wind beneath my wings. Baby got back. It all makes sense now.

6:00 P.M. Pizza, takeout Chinese, or peanut butter? Change diaper.

7:00 P.M. Who is haggard creature in mirror? Brush teeth for first time today.

7:05 P.M. The family walk. Find shoes. Stand outside staring slack-jawed at shrub while husband does everything else. Walk. See neighbors. Neighbors admire Baby. Baby, snug in blanket and cap, looks inscrutable. The daylight is fading. Didn't we just eat breakfast?

8:00 P.M. Husband changes diaper. Husband puts cozy giraffe pajamas on Baby. Husband brings Baby to Mommy. Nurse Baby. Burp Baby. Rock Baby. Watch Baby slip into sleep. Tiptoe to crib and tuck Baby in. Night-night, beautiful Baby. Tell Baby that mommy and daddy are right here. Check baby monitor. Check baby monitor again. Check crib rails. Make sure windows are locked.

9:15 P.M. Collapse onto couch. Tell husband that yes, a movie sounds good. Watch for ten minutes; begin snoring.

11:45 P.M. Husband looming over face. Baby wants mommy. Time to nurse. Baby is hungry. Marvel at how Baby can work up such an appetite. Burp Baby. Chug a bottle of spring water. Stroll back and forth from kitchen to living room, gently rubbing Baby's back. Sing "Old MacDonald," quietly making every animal noise. Change diaper.

1:00 A.M. Crawl into bed. Calculate maximum possible minutes of available sleep. Wonder if it's medically possible for hair to hurt.

4:30 A.M. Please, God; do not let that be Baby crying . . .

Life for a new mommy is a crazy, chaotic, exhausting, messy, and wonderful blur. How to survive it? The keys are low expectations, help that's actually helpful, and decent takeout. Unfortunately, low expectations are an enormous challenge for the Misfit Mom. She's such a perfectionist, such a can-do machine, that the very idea of low expectations makes her skin crawl. She's convinced that with a little organization and enough preparation, even the most difficult newborn will be relatively easy to manage. But there are a few things that she hasn't taken into consideration.

Childbirth takes a serious toll on a woman's body, leaving her weary, depleted, sore, and sometimes—as in the case of a C-section—not fully mobile. Best case scenario: You're tired. Really tired. Worst case scenario: You're spending part of each day holding a bag of frozen peas to a part of your body you never dreamed would yearn for *that* kind of intimate encounter with the Jolly Green Giant.

Sleep deprivation leads to madness. It's a tried and true method of torture. No matter how you feed your baby—breast milk, formula, Ho-Hos—a newborn needs to eat every few hours. There are no easy outs on this. Either you roll over and nurse the baby at 2 A.M., or you get up, heat a bottle, and feed the baby at 2 A.M. Either way, the baby eats and you don't sleep. A few days of broken sleep is rough. A few weeks of broken sleep is painful. A few months of broken sleep and you'll be trying out a new and far less charming personality.

A baby may be only one tiny person, but the load a baby places on your household in terms of laundry, products, responsibility, and

Think You're Tired Now?

Sleep-deprived, sore, delirious—the last thing you feel like doing is going out to eat, right? Well, get moving, sister! Bundle up that baby and head for your favorite restaurant. Very small infants are a pleasure to dine out with compared to their slightly older toddler brethren. A three-month-old will either snooze the meal away in her carrier or be utterly captivated by a rattle, a flickering candle, or the play of light off a window. You will be able to enjoy a leisurely meal and conversation—a combination that will soon be just a memory. The very instant your baby can express an opinion, he or she will. Loudly and insistently. This will almost always be timed to coincide with a meal—*your* meal, that is. When they're not howling, older babies and toddlers like to engage in some or all of the following fun activities in restaurants:

Dump the salt and pepper on the table.

Yank and toss every packet of sweetener within reach.

Transform innocent crackers into hideously mutated crumb-piles.

Pour water/milk/juice onto table and crumb-piles.

Chuck silverware, napkins, and even plates to the floor.

Mash food with their hands, then caress you with those greasy meatloaf mitts.

Burst into screaming tears for no apparent reason.

Not even General Patton could choke down a meal while under siege from a toddler. Trust me: Go out to dinner now, while you still can. Don't wait for a baby-sitter, a reservation, or an occasion. Just go. In a few months you'll be dining in places that boast germ-infested ball pits and surly teenage boys dressed in chicken costumes. Not you? Ha, ha, ha! See you at Chuck E. Cheese!

needs is roughly equal to that of three sloppy, inconsiderate adults. Make that three sloppy, inconsiderate *irrational* adults who have trouble keeping their food down.

If the Misfit Mom isn't careful, she'll be in for a real whipping. There are two things she can do to help herself feel more in control. First, stock the house with two of everything. Since many Misfits already have the useful habit of stockpiling groceries and supplies, this will be a simple and even delightful chore. Go to one of those warehouse stores and load up: diapers, wipes, beverages, nuts, canned soups, soap and laundry detergent, trash bags, etc. Pretend you're hunkering down for a big storm. (You are.)

Second, declutter. Throw away every magazine and catalog. Clean out the refrigerator. Understand that newborn babies are like Pigpen in the Charlie Brown comics. Clouds of merchandise and litter swirl about them: cards, teddy bears, rompers, diapers, wipes, binkies, blankies, and bottles. You won't believe how much stuff a brand-new baby can accumulate. Add a baby's clutter to yours and there won't be any room left in your house for you. It is also in the Misfit Mom's best interest to lower expectations in the following areas:

Your house.

Elle Décor isn't coming by to photograph your living room. So what if it's messy? No one who comes to visit is there to see anything but the baby. Misfits who are secretly hoping to be perceived as the new mother with a spotless house who can effortlessly do it all need to remember that worrying more about dust than about baby leads to Joan Crawford in *Mommie Dearest*. Wire hanger, anyone?

Your marriage.

The romance and cozy friendship will return. Meanwhile, you're both tired, struggling to adapt to your new roles, and feeling like two people gamely trying to bail out a flood with a paper cup. Fatigue makes you snappish and illogical. It can also make you paranoid, quick-tempered, and angry. Not exactly a recipe for closeness. Some couples handle the transition to parenthood beautifully, working harmoniously to balance each other's strengths and shortcomings. Back here on planet earth, you're fuming because your husband is getting a solid six hours of sleep a night and, selfish bastard that he is, will not understand how even the expression on his face can be so insulting to you, the mother of his child. Believe it or not, you're just really, really tired. Exhaustion can easily trick you into thinking that you've married the devil, and now have no recourse but to take your newborn and flee. This is temporary insanity. Postpone all arguments until after you've had a nap. Then send him out to buy you a smoothie and some flowers.

Yourself.

They say it takes the average woman about six weeks to recover from childbirth. Get real and double that. (And be prepared to bleed for a few weeks after giving birth. Tampons aren't permitted, so your baby won't be the only member of the family wearing a diaper.) It can't be said enough: Having a baby is an awesome, momentous physical challenge. You won't feel like your old self for a few months. Be patient. Allow your body all the time it needs to recover. So you can't run a marathon a month after giving birth—what are you supposed to be, the Bionic Woman? Your body has just performed a far more rigorous and miraculous stunt. Give it a break and let it rest. We've all heard about women who give birth and leave the hospital the next day in a pair of size four jeans. Question: Who exactly are these hateful creatures and why do they get so much publicity? Do your mental health a favor and shun these worrisome freaks of nature.

Expect to be more emotional. Some of that *is* hormonal, some of it is part and parcel of falling in love with your new child, and some of it comes from being suddenly thrust into the background of your own life. Out of fear of seeming selfish or immature, very few women will admit to feeling hurt or irritated that their well-being seems hardly to matter to baby-obsessed visitors. One Misfit Mom reported being told, "This is how nature gets you used to the fact that a mother's feelings don't matter." Harsh as that sounds, people do tend to minimize what a mommy goes through in order to bring that perfect baby to the party. While goddesses of old probably fed such fools to the wolves, the modern Misfit Mom has no such satisfying option. She has to play nice. Which brings us to . . .

Helpful help.

Lots of people want to drop by and offer you a hand with the baby. That's beautiful. Here's the problem: There are only so many hands a newborn needs. Frankly, a newborn would infinitely prefer to have mommy or daddy supply all of his feeding, changing, dressing and undressing. That doesn't leave a whole lot for your "helpers" to do—unless they've actually come to help. In that case, there is plenty to go around. Start with dishes, laundry, grocery shopping, cooking, yard work, and pet care. Of course, people who come to see Baby really have no desire to walk Sparky or sort socks. They want to cuddle Baby. That leaves the Misfit Mom three choices:

1. Come right out and ask for help. This is excruciating for the high-achieving, proud, perfectionist Misfit who loathes appearing unable to handle any situation or crisis. Misfits like to give help, not receive it. Plus, the Misfit would rather that no one folded her underwear or t-shirts—not only because they're private, but because no one else is capable of folding

them to her liking. Ditto for grocery shopping—who else could possibly know which brand of whole-grain sticks-and-twigs bread to buy?

2. Play the perfect hostess/complete martyr game. Leap right off the couch, hand the baby to a relative and start taking drink orders. This is the role that Misfits were born and trained for. Making it easy is the fact that contemporary motherhood has come to be defined as a kind of heroic martyrdom, more fit for movie melodrama than reality. She cooks! She cleans! She works full-time! She goes about in rags and never thinks of herself! She's a (sniff) wonderful mother!

3. Make your husband do the dirty work, i.e., assign chores to visitors and usher guests to the door when you and baby have had enough. I confess that this is my preferred method to handle any distasteful task—so much so that my poor husband now complains about always having to be the bad guy. He whines, "I thought you learned about this stuff in therapy." I did—I learned that I'd rather he handled it. Please, a new mother doesn't need any extra stress.

We all know that choice number two is a mistake, leading only to resentment and rage. Playing the martyr is a Misfit's way of maintaining power in a relationship without risking any actual intimacy. Misfits can be martyrs at work ("The unpaid hours I've given this company!"), at home ("You're not the first person to forget my birthday. It's just another day."), and even inside our most secret selves ("I guess I'm one of those people who wasn't meant to be happy."). Investing your energy in reminding others of the many selfless and spectacular things you do for them, all without hope or expectation of thanks, is a losing proposition. What dividends there are end up suffocating everyone involved. Martyrs are not loved, but endured. Seductive as the path to martyrdom is, it leads only to unhappiness. The wise Misfit Mom refuses to be cast in this role. It may be a daily struggle, but she'll fight every minute to avoid becoming a harping dishrag. Start by staying on the couch and letting someone bring *you* a drink. You're not the only person alive who knows how to operate an icemaker.

Choice number three, my personal favorite, is a great big cop-out. I justify it by saying, number one, who just gave birth here? And number two, men like to be useful. It's in their very nature to puff themselves up and make scary noises to protect their families. There may be some truth to that but my poor husband has been played off as the bad cop so many times that he's developing a complex. Deep down we all know that choice number one is the right way to go. Frank and open communication is the bulwark of a healthy and happy life. Since articulating a need or a weakness can be so scary for the Misfit, it's only sensible to start small. Allow yourself to be vulnerable to the person you trust most—your husband. Be brave and tell him what you need: rest and time with your baby. With luck, he'll interpret that as a call to action and get his mother to unload the dishwasher. If he doesn't respond to the subtle approach, pull him aside, fix him with your most menacing psycho stare, and hiss, "Either put those people to work or get them out of here, or I will never stop screaming." Be sure to flare your nostrils a little. That's always spooky. There—you've expressed a need! That wasn't so hard, was it? Can we all agree that a little progress is better than none at all?

A helping hand is a lovely thing indeed, especially when it's fetching you a cold lemonade and inquiring as to your wishes for dinner. But understand: A houseful of helpers also means an earful of advice. Some of it will be good, some great, and some of it completely unrealistic, not to mention absolutely aggravating. Classic tidbits include:

Sleep when the baby sleeps.

This makes all the sense in the world, but it's a tough one to live by. You will want to groom, eat, exercise, talk, think, read, have a marriage, have sex, shop, and pay bills. You'll be surprised to discover how hard a baby makes any one of these to accomplish, which is why you'll rush to fit the above in while baby is napping. You'll also try doing many of the things on the above list while the baby is awake, but with mixed results.

Although there are a number of very good baby containment/distraction devices on the market, baby will not appreciate being strapped into a swing or bouncy seat every time he's finished eating. Babies like to be held, and have an amusing way of shrieking like little car alarms to let you know it. Also, while they may seem like pudgy blobs, in reality, babies are extremely curious and hardworking individuals who rely on you to introduce them to the world. They are incapable of understanding that you have other needs or obligations to tend to. The fact that they seem to desperately require your attention the very instant you lift the phone, a fork, or a toilet seat lid is merely a freaky coincidence.

Ready for a more realistic interpretation? If baby's awake, you'll be busy. When baby's asleep, you'll have stuff you want to do. The answer is to sleep when you can and just expect to get less accomplished. Most things can wait while you adjust to your new life and schedule. So the house is dusty? The latest research into asthma and allergies indicates that children who grow up in an environment with some dust, pet hair, and typical household dirt are less likely to experience allergic reactions to those things. What better proof could you want that being a hysterical clean-freak perfectionist is bad for your health?

Babies cry to exercise their lungs.

Babies cry for a variety of reasons: hunger, cold, fatigue, pain, distress, and the discomfort of a full diaper. Babies have only needs, not demands, and are incapable of manipulating or deliberately tormenting their parents. Crying is the only way a baby can communicate those needs. Which means, a crying baby *needs* something. It might be as simple as a good burp, or it might be the less tangible but infinitely more rewarding comfort of your touch. There are good studies indicating that babies whose parents respond to their needs (cries) promptly are blessed with babies who cry less frequently. Those babies feel secure and confident. A baby who howls itself blue while your mother-in-law sits in the next room telling you, "Don't go in there. She's trying to train you," is a baby who is rapidly learning that her needs won't be met.

Older women will tell you how they used to stand outside their nurseries listening to their babies wail. Those women, often in tears, had to force themselves to ignore those increasingly desperate cries, while every instinct they had screamed to do just the opposite. Does that make sense to you? To leave a helpless, anguished being alone in a room to prove that you won't be "trained" to respond to his or her cries?

Ready for a more realistic interpretation? Mommies respond to babies—that's our job. Crying is how a baby communicates. Show your baby that you're listening by going to her when she screams. The only babies capable of plotting against their parents star in grade B horror movies. In real life, a peaceful, secure baby equals a peaceful, secure mommy. Never apologize or defend yourself to anyone who is critical of how you nurture your infant. And always remember to take any advice offered by the same people who raised you with a really big grain of salt.

Cereal will make the baby sleep.

An entire generation of mothers believed fervently in the power of Gerber cereal to knock out even the most miserably wakeful baby. These desperate creatures would fill a baby bottle with a formula/cereal mixture, then take a pin or knife tip and widen the opening on the nipple to allow the soupy brew to flow down baby's gullet. These women, also known as our mothers, swore by this method. Many of us, half crazed with fatigue, have followed in their footsteps. There are a couple of things to consider before taking this step. First, babies aren't born with mature digestive systems, and giving cereal too early can lead to all sorts of problems. A baby simply cannot digest large amounts of food at a single sitting. That's just the way they're built, and force-feeding won't hurry it along.

Introducing certain foods too early can also increase the risk of food allergies, for example, to wheat or rice. Add constipation, which is a horrible thing for a little one to endure, and you begin to see why pediatricians discourage the feeding of solids until somewhere around month four. My daughter was such a round-the-clock wakeful baby that it would have taken a prime rib and a martini just to slow her down, and no amount of cereal in her diet bought us even one additional minute of sleep. Food is not necessarily the answer to the question "Why isn't the baby sleeping?"

Ready for a more realistic interpretation? Hunger is not the only thing that disrupts a baby's sleep cycle. Some babies sleep for ten hours at a stretch; others snooze for a maximum of four. Breast-fed babies, with their more frequent feedings, are particular targets for the well-intentioned baby nutrition cops who lurk in every family. Nursing moms should brace themselves for an onslaught of "you're starving that poor thing!" A tired and hormonal Misfit, upon hearing the words *poor*, *thing*, and *starving*, will be beside herself with guilt, doubt, and self-recrimination. That's when it's time to pick up the phone and talk to your pediatrician. Do this before starting your baby on solids, and don't be surprised if he or she refuses to endorse the cereal-spiked bottle plan. Most doctors want you to feed cereal with a spoon, not a nipple. Maybe they learn this sort of thing at med school? As opposed to, oh I don't know, the bowling alley bar where your aunt Arlene apparently picked up so many of her tips?

If you nurse that baby, you'll never be able to leave the house.

The breast-feeding mom is not under house arrest. In fact, nursing moms actually have a somewhat easier time taking baby out into the world—no bottles, no worries. All a nursing mom needs is a few clean diapers and a blanket and she can go just about anywhere. That's the beauty of breast milk; it's always fresh, always the perfect temperature, and you can't possibly forget to pull it out of the fridge.

Nursing an infant in public is a relatively simple thing, requiring no special equipment or accommodation. Although you can buy blouses designed specifically for nursing mothers, you may be more comfortable wearing regular clothes. Nursing blouses generally have either a flap, pleat, or ruffle concealing horizontal slits at the breast. Couple that with the snaps and hooks of a nursing bra and believe me, you'll spend more time fumbling with your chest than the average fifteen-year-old boy. Forcing an unwieldy and temporarily gigantic breast through one of those openings can be more of an unwelcome attention-getter than nursing itself. I ended up just wearing my usual t-shirts and blouses—and regular bras. When I needed to feed my daughter, whether at a restaurant or a park, I simply reached under my shirt, freed my breast, and lifted her to it. The shirt concealed all but her face, and her body and blanket covered what little of my tummy might be exposed. Easy and painless.

It always makes me sad to see other moms sitting in restaurants with blankets over their heads, or trying to nurse their babies while crouched on toilet seats in the ladies' room. That's just plain wrong. Nursing is a regular, healthy part of life, and can be practiced with enough discretion to make everyone present comfortable—including mother and baby. I was so determined never to feed my child on a public toilet that, in typical Misfit spirit, I printed out a copy of my state's breast-feeding legislation and carried it in my handbag. I was just itching for a fight! I never got one. In fact, I never got so much as a curious glance, and I nursed my child from one side of the country to the other in every imaginable situation. When it comes to successful breast-feeding, attitude is everything. A nursing mom who is comfortable and relaxed can feed her baby in public without making a big deal of it. As for leaving the house without baby, that's what breast pumps are for. Bottom line: Don't let yourself be talked out of nursing if you want to do it.

Constant holding spoils the baby.

I'm going to have to be very blunt: This is crazy talk. Holding, caressing, snuggling, rocking, kissing, squeezing, and cuddling your baby is one of the most joyful, wonderful, comforting, pleasurable experiences available to us as human beings. Babies adore being touched, but more than that, they *need* to be touched. Babies who are not touched and held can suffer devastating physical and emotional consequences. It's called *failure to thrive*, and it's a serious, heartbreaking reality for children who are deprived of regular physical contact with a parent or caregiver, for example, babies institutionalized in orphanages. Babies need cuddling the same way they need food and water. It's essential. Period. It's life affirming and healing. And it's *fun*.

For the Misfit Mom who has yearned for real, unconditional love her whole life, the experience of caring for her newborn is balm to her mistrustful heart. To brush your lips against a baby's tender cheek, to feel her sweet milky breath on your neck, is to taste a little bit of heaven. For the Misfit, always self-conscious, anxious, and afraid, the physical reality of her own infant child offers a wondrous opportunity to relax and live fully in the moment. Feel the warm, pleasurable weight of your baby lying on your chest. Curl up on the couch and discover how perfectly your baby's head nestles into the curve between your chin and shoulder. Rub your baby's back and legs. Some mommies swear that their babies just about purr with happiness while being cuddled. You'll want to purr, too. Don't deny yourself or your child a single nuzzle. When it comes to hugs, more is always better.

Ready for a more realistic interpretation? Love doesn't spoil a baby—substitutes for love do. Never expect a stuffed animal or toy to deliver the comfort of a mommy's arms. Cherish every minute your baby spends in your lap. Soon, he or she will be grown up and gone. Then, when you're old and living in a refrigerator box beneath an overpass, you'll wish your baby were tiny again. Okay, so maybe you won't be living in a cardboard box. But you *will* long for the days when you held your precious baby in your arms. That's a promise.

Forget all this newfangled nonsense—babies sleep better on their stomachs.

How, when, where, and how much baby sleeps will become the driving issue in your life. The loud and insistent opinions you were bludgeoned with over what you fed your baby were just a dress rehearsal for the real show: baby's bedtime. Conventional wisdom used to be that a baby who slept on its back might choke to death on its own vomit, so babies were routinely put to sleep on their tummies. Then medical experts decided that no, it was safest to put babies on their backs to sleep, with no blankets, pillows or toys in the crib. No wonder parents are mystified—it seems that every generation is handed a new set of standards to follow. When we were infants, we were probably put to sleep on our stomachs. Many of us were tucked into makeshift beds in dresser drawers or laundry baskets and did just fine.

Infant sleep practices are much studied and scrutinized. It's not just about making sure that babies and parents get enough rest, but to lessen the risk of SIDS (Sudden Infant Death Syndrome). SIDS is the single greatest fear haunting new parents. Experts do not know what causes SIDS, but theories range from an overwhelming reaction to bacteria in crib mattresses, to genetic anomalies, to suffocation. SIDS is a tragic, devastating unknown, and medical experts are frantic to find answers. Until then, all we can do is follow the advice of those experts and put our babies on their backs to sleep. Think of all that fancy crib bedding and those adorable stuffed toys as strictly decorative for now. Warm, close-fitting pajamas are all baby needs at bedtime. Just make sure that baby gets plenty of tummy time while awake. Tummy time helps build and strengthen the muscles needed for sitting up and crawling—and crawling is linked to reading, of all things. A mother's work is never done! But look on the bright side: By the time you're a grandmother, we'll probably be suspending infants from their ankles at bedtime like tiny bats. Then you'll be the one to shake your head and drone on about how things used to be done. That's something to look forward to, isn't it?

If you sleep with the baby, it will a) smother or b) remain in your bed until it leaves home.

Cosleeping is one of the most controversial parenting practices on earth. There is a tremendous amount of passion on both sides of the issue. Many cosleeping families keep it a secret, rather than be harangued and criticized for their choice. My husband and I kept our daughter in our bed until she was ten months old, at which time she moved to a crib in her own room. (Believe it or not, the transition was smooth and problem-free.) Why did we do it? Our reasons at first were pragmatic. After a difficult labor and a C-section complicated by severe blood loss, I needed a lot of rest and as much help with nursing as possible.

For her first two weeks, Olivia and I spent much of the day in bed, drowsing, chatting, making faces at each other, and nursing. It seemed weird to suddenly relocate her at "bedtime" just because the sun had gone down. Although we'd never planned or discussed it, my husband and I looked at each other and realized that keeping her with us simply felt right. To our surprise, we were a bed-sharing family. It was only after mentioning our decision on the radio that I discovered how many complete strangers disagreed with us. Some violently. I wasted a lot of energy trying to explain the logic behind our choice—and I say *wasted* because, as you'll soon discover, disagreements over childrearing practices can get so heated that they'd end up in fistfights if the participants weren't too tired to take it outside.

We looked at it this way: Human beings are the only animals that abandon their young at night. For someone so small and new to be all alone in another room just felt wrong. Then we did some homework and found that advocates of cosleeping argue that close proximity to the mother helps the infant regulate respiration and temperature. Cosleeping also facilitates breast-feeding and enables nursing moms to get more and better sleep. There is also persuasive data indicating that the rate of SIDS is substantially lower to nonexistent in cultures where cosleeping is the norm. As for turning baby into a clinging vine, cosleepers claim that babies kept close at night develop a greater sense of security and as a result ultimately grow into more independent children.

It all made good sense to us, so out went our mountain of pillows and in came our baby daughter. She slept on her back between us, at the head of our pillowless king-size bed. Neither of us ever rolled over on her or knocked her onto the floor. If anything, we fought over who got to cuddle her last before drifting off to sleep each night. We'll always treasure the memory of waking up so many mornings to her plump and beaming face. It was a blissful, happy experience. It worked beautifully for us for ten months, at which time Little Miss Squirmy moved into her own crib and room where she has happily slept through the night ever since. We're not weirdos, freaks, or spooky crunchy people. We're just regular parents who made a choice that worked for our family. You have that same right.

If you do opt to cosleep, do your homework and make sure that your sleeping environment is up to snuff for an infant. Check out some of the products designed for cosleeping, including terrific little bassinet-type things that hook directly to the edge of your mattress. That may be the best of both worlds—baby safely tucked away in her own bed, but at arm's reach all night long. Also keep in mind that bed-sharing families cannot be blotto on booze or wasted on pills. Those behaviors do place your baby at significant risk of being harmed or suffocated while in your bed. Of course, the Misfit Mom knows first-hand that substance abuse is a bad strategy for raising kids regardless of where in the house you put them to sleep.

Although I've learned the hard way that talking about cosleeping is an invitation to aggravation, I feel compelled to come clean. There are too many Misfit Moms who barely sleep for the first couple of months of their children's lives. Why? Because they are so anxious and keyed up about the baby's welfare that they tiptoe back and forth from the crib to their room all night long just to make sure the baby is breathing. How many nights can you spend watching an infant's chest rise and fall or listening to every sound the baby monitor makes before you go insane? That kind of anxiety interferes with your quality of life, your health, your marriage, and can greatly diminish your joy in motherhood. If worries about the baby keep you awake and churning, then put your baby—crib and all, if need be—in your bedroom and be done with it. Who cares what anybody else thinks? You're the mommy now, and you really do know best.

Here you are: a month or so into motherhood and already you've learned so many things. You've discovered that there's much more to late-night television than ads for "Girls Gone Wild." You've realized that, until recently, you had no idea what *tired*, *busy*, or *overwhelmed* really meant. You can't quite remember how you used to fill your days, but your old life now seems one of ridiculous ease and leisure. Your whole sense of time has been altered. Before, each day lined up in your mind as neat and orderly as soldiers awaiting inspection. Now, time flows unchecked over and around you, leaving you stunned and sputtering at its rapid passage. That eight-week maternity leave, the one you envisioned as an idyllic mommy-baby vacation complete with shopping, dining at outdoor cafes, and long, luxurious naps, is flying by, and you've hardly left the house. You're still wearing maternity clothes—something you vowed not to do—and don't even ask about the finer points of grooming. With fatigue making you feel as though your eyeballs have been boiled in acid, it's hard to muster much enthusiasm for a good eyebrow waxing. Though you'll begin each day swearing to be extremely organized and efficient, things will have an annoying tendency to get away from you by lunchtime. All it takes is one leaking, explosive diaper to derail an entire morning. Don't be alarmed if you find yourself slumped on the floor crying wretched tears over your inability to locate your other shoe. It's normal, and so are you.

Um, Isn't That for Jock Itch?

Let's say you've been nursing for a few weeks now and thought that everything was going fine. That is, until you wake up one morning with red, flaky, itchy or burning nipples accompanied by a sharp, shooting pain that radiates from the nipple during or after a feeding. Has your baby become a carnivorous predator who must immediately be weaned? Do you have some horrifyingly rare disease in your breasts? The answer is no and no. What you have is most likely *thrush*, which is a kind of yeast infection. You caught it from your baby, who has it in his or her mouth. (Note: Bottle babies get thrush, too, so keep an eye on your little one. Many babies aren't bothered by it, but some are made cranky and fussy— and will show their irritation at feeding time.) If you think thrush may be the culprit, take a peek inside baby's mouth. Look for milky white deposits inside the cheeks and on the tongue. If that white stuff is milk, you can wipe if off. If you can't, it's probably thrush. Treatment is simple. Your pediatrician will prescribe an antifungal medication that you'll swab the baby's mouth with. You'll also want to throw away or boil any binkies or rubber nipples that you've been using to prevent reinfection. As for you, after nursing, make sure your nipples are clean and dry, then apply a thin coat of an antifungal cream containing *clotrimazole*. You'll find it in the drugstore under a variety of brand names including Cruex (*Cures the itch!*), best known as a remedy for that sexy affliction called jock itch. Other brands containing the same ingredient promise to cure athlete's foot or ringworm. I know, I know—it's gross even to think about. As unsavory as it is, try to remember that pregnancy and virtually all of motherhood is designed to beat the last bit of squeamishness out of us, transforming us into mighty warrior moms who can face anything a kid can throw our way. If smearing jock itch cream on your boobs is too awful for you to contemplate, then maybe you should have found a glass slipper and a ticket to the ball, Cinderella. There are far nastier things ahead than a little Cruex on your cleavage. Trust me.

Having always held herself to impossibly lofty standards, the Misfit is used to cruising at altitudes that leave other mortals breathless. Yet like Icarus flying too close to the sun on his waxen wings, the Misfit who becomes a mommy almost can't help but plummet back to earth. This is one fall the Misfit shouldn't fear. Real motherhood, with all its pleasures and pains, happens on the ground, not in the clouds. A real mommy isn't some manufactured fantasy of selflessness and domestic engineering. A real mommy gets her hands (and her clothes and her house) dirty doing the job. A real mommy is *you*, with all of your worries and mistakes and imperfections, and not the idea you had in your head of how magically wonderful everything would be. So another day has melted away and you're still in your pajamas? So what? You've got more important things to do. Like chewing on your baby's feet—a delightful pastime so addictive that it ought to be packaged and sold to the masses. Forget gummy bears! There's nothing more fun than munching on tiny piggy toes while your baby squeals in delight. It may be one of the last great things you can put in your mouth that won't make you fat or get you into trouble. A plump little baby foot—I still swoon at the thought of it! Chomp while you can, because nothing this sweet is meant to last.

10

That Other Job

The day dawns faster than you ever dreamed. Eight weeks ago you were still pregnant, childless, and unable to imagine yourself as a mommy. Now your old life beckons, but it's a whole new you that answers the call. Waking up to an alarm clock feels strange and, worse, cruel—especially if you haven't been getting much sleep at night. Before you roll out of bed and stumble through your usual morning routine, stop and consider this: Your usual morning routine is gone forever. In addition to getting yourself showered, dressed, fed, packed up, and out the door, you now have a baby to tend to. Depending on what sort of child care arrangements you've made, that baby will have to be dressed, fed, and packed up as well.

Remember the old commercial for the armed services that bragged, "We get more done by eight A.M. than most people do all day"? One army that can honestly bellow that particular battle cry is the Working Mom Army. Recruits in this platoon routinely do a load of laundry before dawn, feed sleepy babies with one hand, and march out the door with a static-cling sock hiding in their sleeve. They then storm the office or factory or retail kiosk, and spend the entire day trying to prove that motherhood hasn't reduced their efficiency or dedication one iota. Many working moms feel pressure to prove that they're still hungry, ambitious, focused. Fatigue, or sorrow and ambivalence over leaving their children in the care of another, must be carefully concealed or left in the parking lot outside. That women are still required to play out this little charade is a load of crap bigger than any you'll find in a diaper, but it's the unspoken reality of the workplace. Welcome back to the job, Misfit Mom.

There are some things I will never understand. For instance, why are women, famed for our verbal gifts and love of conversation, so woefully absent from the top positions in talk radio? What is talk radio, after all, but talk? Isn't talking what we're forever doing, according to our fans and critics alike? And why are pregnant women treated like large, bumbling, slow-witted children who want nothing more than to be garbed in smocks festooned with kitties and butterflies? And why, oh why, are working women so often relegated to the sidelines, whether of power or paycheck, once they become mothers?

If we were smart enough to recognize the additional skills a working mom brings to the table, mommies would be running every major corporation in the country—and probably the government as well. Working moms are masters at juggling conflicting tasks and needs. They're skilled at sorting and prioritizing. Working moms practically invented multitasking, and are wizards at improvising solutions and managing schedules. Put a Misfit Mom in charge and you've got an absolute can-do machine to keep everything humming. But no, this isn't how it works. Instead, a working mom can expect to be viewed with some suspicion—I once actually heard a manager say of a coworker, "Oh, with her, family always comes first." Hello? Like pricing widgets for X Corp. should be her highest priority? Or anyone else's for that matter? A working mom can also expect to be chastised if her child is sick, and that sickness interrupts mommy's work day. She can expect to be judged severely for taking time off for doctor appointments, school visits, or snow days.

There is actually a company in Pennsylvania that forbids the placement of personal photographs on desks or in cubicles for fear, I presume, that the very sight of their families might be too distracting for the mostly female workforce. If this sounds nuts, it should. Human beings shouldn't be required to sacrifice their souls and lives in the name of business getting done, but doing exactly that has sadly become a too common job requirement. And if you think the old double standard no longer applies, then you're to be commended for your idealism, if not your grasp of reality. Working men with families are called *employees*; working women with families are called *working mothers*. Guess which carries more baggage? At a time in our history when the phrase *family values* is puked up by one politico or another on a daily basis, it's almost laughable to note just how low the value our culture places on the family really is. In fact, the phrase *family values* is sometimes used more to chastise women who combine career and children than it is to describe a system of beliefs or practices. The message, whether subtle or blatant, is that many of the problems haunting our society today have their roots in women leaving the home. That's an awfully heavy burden for anyone to carry—yet working moms shoulder it every single morning.

Much has been made of the conflict that has raged between working and stay-at-home mothers over the last twenty-five or thirty years. Watching women argue with other women over who has made the morally superior choice for her family has provided a handy distraction from the real issues of compensation, affordable health coverage, child care, family leave, and simple economic need. Having discussed this issue countless times on our radio program for the past ten years, I've heard it all. Women work for "extras" like designer clothes and BMWs. Feminism has destroyed the family. Women have forgotten their proper place in society as taught in the Bible. The liberal media preaches a homosexual, antifamily, antireligion agenda. I've heard from women who stay home that working women are selfish and unworthy, and from working women that those who stay home are judgmental and unrealistic. From meat-headed buffoons like Newt Gingrich who preached a righteous old-fashioned morality to us while practicing a far less savory version himself, to strident harpies like Dr. Laura Schlessinger with her rigid sermonizing about a mother's duty, working women have been brutally whipped for years. It's time to say *enough*.

Women, like the proverbial genie, won't be shoved back into the bottle. We go to school, we vote, we have jobs—and we have families. This is reality. That same reality includes an ever-escalating cost of living and a fifty percent divorce rate. Not every family looks like a Norman Rockwell painting—in fact, very few do. Many argue (and I think I've heard from each of them personally) that all of this negative societal change is a direct result of women's embrace of feminism. Yes, women have changed—and so have men, and the economy, and the culture, and the world itself, for that matter. Call it progress, history, the march of time—just understand that it only moves forward. Forcing women back into the starched and idealized world of the 1950s can't magically undo the last half century. Nor should we seek that. After all, if the 1950s were such a bastion of healthy and harmonious family values, then why was that glorified decade followed by the wrenching upheaval of the 1960s?

What is often overlooked is the fact that women have *always* worked. Donna Reed, vacuuming in her pearls and heels, is a recent invention. From planting to piecework, domestic service to dictation, women have been in the workforce for virtually all of recorded history. In fact, not only did women go to work, kids did too. The modern notion of childhood as a prolonged period of nurture and enchantment was practically invented at roughly the same time we started making noises about how a woman's place was in the home. Children used to spend their days laboring on family farms or worse, under brutal and dangerous conditions in factories and sweatshops. No one in their right mind would advocate a return to those grim times. (Except maybe my sister-in-law, who, after raising five kids, strongly believes that a stint in a dirty factory might have taught her lot to whine a little less about having to make their own beds.) Maybe the real challenge doesn't lie in figuring out whether or not women *should* work, but in asking ourselves why it is we've so devalued women's labor—particularly childrearing—that it took a slew of women burning their bras and racing for the corporate high-rise to make us think that women worked at all. Just what do we think women have been doing for the past thirty-five thousand years? Playing Bunco? Guess again. Women work.

Waxing poetic about the past does nothing to address the conflicts and challenges faced by today's working parents. No woman should ever be required to justify why she works or for how much, to anyone. Those are personal choices, not campaign planks or promises. It is loathsome to judge working mothers, who care deeply about the welfare of their children, by the kind of harsh and unforgiving standards that so often apply. Just because a mother works outside the home, it doesn't mean she loves her children any less. It doesn't mean she's less interested in their intellectual development, or more careless of their emotional needs. It doesn't mean she's selfish. Listen to the tone of those who chastise women who combine families and careers. It's smug, superior, even a little haughty. "She shouldn't complain," they say. "She knew the job. Should have thought about that before she had kids." Doesn't that reasoning sound awfully familiar? Doesn't it remind you a bit of *she asked for it?* It's amazing: we've dressed that weary old chestnut up in new clothes, only to hang it over the heads of working mothers. No wonder we're all so tired. The reality is, some mommies go to work. Get over it. As a listener once succinctly noted, "Yeah, I work for extras. Extra food, extra heat, and extra clothes on my kid's back."

Whatever you're working for, your first weeks back on the job will be strange. Maternity leave gave you a taste of baby time—a clock- and calendar-free blur. That makes going back to a regimented sched- ule tough. Then there are the intangible baby issues to be dealt with. It's often only after a new mommy returns to work and is away from her infant that she realizes how her thoughts are dominated by con- cerns for her baby. What is Baby doing now? Is she eating? Is she cry- ing? The work at hand seems petty and trivial compared to these worries. This is when the anti-mommy faction whispers, "She's lost her edge."

If all of us—male and female—were absolutely honest, we'd admit that a great deal of the work we do *is* petty and trivial and not nearly as important as it's made out to be. Sure, the wheels of commerce must turn and all that, but to a new mommy, it seems pretty silly. I'm with the new mommies. It's normal to feel this way—think of it as a bio- logically wired-in survival mechanism. If humans had not evolved to place utmost priority on the care and tending of the young, our species would have died out long ago. That's not to say that we should all make a beeline for the nearest cave and get back to simple, club- wielding basics. But new mommies today struggle to find their way in

Baby Fun Fact!

Your infant will catch a cold. Even if you hardly ever leave the house, breast-feed, eat only organic produce, and compulsively wash your hands twenty times a day. There's a reason they call it the common cold—it's, well, common. Once baby is snuffling and miserable and feverish, you'll be sorely tempted to rush to the drugstore and buy one of the various products labeled "Infant Cold Drops." Before you do, know this: that particular remedy may make your baby wakeful and excitable. "Excitable" sounds cute, but in the real world it means hopped up, crabby, and absolutely unable to sleep. Unfortunately, you will not fully grasp the magnitude of this potential side effect until after you've spent a thoroughly desperate and sleepless night with your sick baby. Who knows why some babies react this way to infant cold drops? And at 3 A.M. who really cares? You just want to go to bed—after all, you have to go to work in the morning. You can't function without sleep, and no one at work or at home wants to listen to you whine about how exhausted you feel. Upon hearing of your wild infant-cold-remedy all-nighter, even your pediatrician will simply nod sagely and say, "That happens. Next time, stick to Tylenol. Do you have a humidifier?" Moral of the story: Read all labels very carefully—and to be safe, assume you'll be stuck with any and all negative side effects.

a vortex of emotions, desires, conflicting responsibilities, and mixed messages about what it means to be a woman—and a mother.

One unforeseen casualty of the progress we've enjoyed over the last four decades is the splintering of family and community, leaving many women without adequate support or assistance. No wonder so many mothers suffer from post-partum depression. They feel overwhelmed and worse, unequal to the task at hand. Having been deluged with images of chic, competent mothers with briefcases in one hand and newborns in the other, many women are totally unprepared for the reality of blending work and family. It's harder, lonelier, and more exhausting than they ever dreamed. Most working mothers are pulled by a fierce undertow of duty and longing, of obligation and expectation. There is always a voice whispering: "Maybe you should have thought about that before having a baby." Working mothers are judged—and judge themselves—every single day for the choices they've made. That's not to say working fathers don't experience similar conflicts between job and family. They do. The difference is, working fathers are not assumed to have had a *choice* in the matter. It's on that perceived choice that virtually the entire debate between working and nonworking mothers pivots. If a mother doesn't "need" to work, should she? And who gets to decide the threshold of need?

The decision to work outside the home isn't always about money. Sometimes it's about fulfillment. Here's a subject that everyone tiptoes around, because to suggest that staying home with children is anything less than nirvana is to be labeled a bad mother. One mother of two, a physician, told me, "I feel judged sometimes. You know, why am I off taking care of other people while my own children are with a sitter? You do feel guilty. But I love being a doctor. It's what I've always wanted. And I hope my daughters see that anything is possible for them, too." The effort to balance work and home, while simultaneously trying to justify the decision to have kids *and* a job is what makes the entire debate such fertile ground for guilt, blame, and name-calling. What kind of woman takes a job just because she craves contact with other adults? What kind of woman secretly confesses to being driven mad by the endless repetitions of Teletubbies and Barney? What kind of woman dares to think that she might earn a paycheck and raise a family at the same time? Without the world crashing down around her? The answer is, a real woman. Not a statistic, not a commodity to be analyzed by pollsters and politicians. A real woman. The kind you see every day at the grocery store, the bank, and the gas station. Does she look like an evil harpy hell-bent on wrecking the institution of the family? Or does she look sort of like, well, you? While the argument over when, why, and how much women should work rages over our heads, real women simply get on with the business of living. Some pursue a career. Some raise a family. Some do both. So who gets to decide what "need" is? You do. It's up to you and your partner—*your* family values, in other words. Just as biology alone can't make you a good mommy, your decision to hold a job or not won't seal your children's fate either. It's what you do with your choice that truly matters. Let the pundits nitpick and bicker—all over this country Misfit Moms are getting the job done.

A year's worth of business planning went into my pregnancy. A six-week maternity leave was unthinkable. No one in radio can take that much time off these days and expect to have a job to return to. The decision was made to buy enough gear to allow me to broadcast the show from home. That was one problem solved. Business travel would be suspended for the last trimester of my pregnancy, and resumed five weeks after the baby's birth—with the understanding that the baby would accompany me on every trip for at least her first year. This way, I could work, travel, and still continue to breast-feed. With the battle plan in place, and a positive pregnancy test (or six) in hand, we went public with the news.

The reaction was an eye-opener. Letters of support and encouragement poured in from listeners. Handmade baby blankets, booties, and other gifts piled up—all with good wishes from strangers who felt part of our radio family. The industry, however, reacted a little differently. A prominent broadcast consultant informed us flatly that pregnancy was a ratings killer, that *female* listeners hated it. Some affiliate stations expressed concern that the show was going to become "some kind of gynecology baby, baby, baby thing." I wasn't exactly surprised—I'd been told by another radio consultant at the beginning of my career that I was sure to be a failure because "women don't like other women." (This bit of wisdom came as real news to me since I'd been under the lifelong delusion that women were capable of close, enduring friendships.) I'd also worked long enough in radio to have no illusions about how women are perceived or treated. Female radio consumers have been neatly divided by the industry into young, tattooed, pierced party girls who want to hear lots of the latest hit music; and bubble-bath-taking, minivan-driving soccer moms who cringe at any controversy and want to hear lots of soft, "lite" favorites. The "experts" apparently believe that no one in either camp has ever had a female friend, a child, or puzzled out exactly where it is babies come from.

Like all Misfits who are used to shrugging off doubters and critics, I forged ahead with my pregnancy—and guess what? Ratings went up. Maybe talking about my brand-new double D-cup breasts brought in male listeners. Or maybe, just maybe, pregnancy is a normal part of life that doesn't scare normal people away. That it spooks a bunch of hopelessly dorky radio guys who had to dream up fake names like John St. John and Rick Speed just to get dates tells you everything you need to know about those kind of guys—and about the radio business.

I gave birth, took a whopping three weeks to recover from my C-section, and was back on the air like nothing had ever happened. I worked in my pajamas with my sleeping baby in my lap. When she needed to eat, I nursed her on-air without missing a beat. (Actual question from a programming executive: "Won't it be disgusting to hear her nurse that baby?" He apparently feared that a nursing infant might snort and slurp like a hog at a trough.) Olivia was fed once or twice per broadcast and no one was the wiser. At five weeks I bundled her up, climbed aboard a small jet, and flew off to Wisconsin to host a charity golf tournament. So what if I was pale, anemic, and in a near-hallucinatory state of fatigue? The show must go on—and it did.

I had an ulterior motive for trying so hard. Like all Misfits, I had something to prove. No woman in my company had ever been permitted to work from home before. The last thing I wanted to do was slack off and possibly ruin a good thing for the next mom in line. For years, I'd heard stories of women who'd resigned in their last trimesters when their job-sharing, flextime, or telecommuting proposals were rejected; I felt a little guilty to be receiving special treatment. (Fun way to kill time: Add up all the things you feel "a little" guilty about. When the sum total becomes too crushing to bear, pour a glass of red wine, lie on the couch, and watch a chick movie on cable. Here's a good one: *You've Got Mail*. Only in Hollywood will you find a woman who moons over some guy she's met on the Internet while a perfectly adorable Greg Kinnear is living *right there* with her in a fabulous New York apartment. Is there no pleasing Meg Ryan?) To demonstrate my extreme professionalism, I adhered to the following schedule:

3:45 A.M. Wake up, nurse baby.

4:10 A.M. Wash face, brush teeth, scowl at hair.

4:30 A.M. Eat breakfast (two eggs, decaf tea). Fantasize about a steaming Starbucks.

4:45 A.M. Turn on CNN; head outside to fetch newspaper.

5:00 A.M. Scan Internet for important news, i.e., newly deceased or arrested celebrities.

5:30 A.M. Dial up main air studio, check in with producers.

5:40 A.M. Bob arrives. Hiss at dogs to be quiet.

6:00 A.M. First hour of the broadcast.

7:00 A.M. Second hour of the broadcast. Bob whines about needing breakfast.

8:00 A.M. Third hour of broadcast. Nurse baby. Bob, who was at first mortified with embarrassment at whole breast-feeding concept, and would hide in the next room for fear of seeing something that might instantly cause him to go mad, is now a blasé old hand. He crawls around on the floor and plays with Olivia during commercials.

9:00 A.M. Final hour of broadcast.

10:00 A.M. Record liners*, commercials, and promotional announcements for affiliate stations.

10:45 A.M. Bob leaves.

11:00 A.M. Return phone calls, answer mail, prep show for next day.

12:00 NOON. Quitting time.

Working at home was fabulous, but it wasn't exactly a vacation. No one in his or her right mind wakes up at 3:45 A.M. I think even dairy farmers get a little more shut-eye than that. After about six weeks of this, with only a few hours of uninterrupted sleep at night, I was starting to become demented. Words would get tangled up in my mouth and come out sounding like gibberish. No longer able to keep track of dates or times, I'd become hopelessly paralyzed by requests for meetings or appearances. Bleary and confused, I was provoked to tears by the slightest thing. Yet every morning I fired up that microphone, uncrossed my bloodshot eyes, and slogged forward, determined to prove that having a baby hadn't taken anything off my fastball.

I also began making insane wardrobe choices, although that can be

---

*A liner is radio-speak for the on-air statements used by stations to deliver their marketing or format position. For example, "You're listening to Bob and Sheri on Zippy 100— your home for today's hottest music!"

more directly attributed to the Mirage of Post-Partum Thinness. This treacherous trap snares many a Misfit Mom. Here's how it works: Shortly before giving birth you will feel as huge and unwieldy as a beached whale. It will be an effort to stand, move, or even breathe. Immediately after giving birth, you will feel impossibly thin, bony, perhaps even waiflike. Flushed with relief at no longer being enormous, and giddy with what you perceive to be your newly svelte form, you will be tempted to tart yourself up in something slinky and revealing. Don't. I actually left the house in a short, cut-on-the-bias lavender skirt and fitted sleeveless blouse not three weeks after being discharged from the hospital. I felt light as air and absolutely emaciated. How I looked, on the other hand, was like one of the ballerina hippos in *Fantasia*. Don't be fooled. In fact, if this were a just world, new mommies would all be issued a temporary insanity pass granting us amnesty from all rules of social conduct, emotional restraint, and, of course, fashion.

Demented, deluded, and struggling to keep my brand-new motherhood from affecting my job performance in any way, I finally understood why so many women I'd known had thrown in the towel and just quit working. A mommy has plenty to do without taking on anything else. Especially a job, which, like most of adult life, has more in common with high school than any of us ever dreamed. Your single, childless coworkers are like the affluent popular kids: carefree, with few obligations and nothing but good times to look forward to. Instead of parties after the game, they congregate for drinks outside the office. The working mommy might like to go too, but she's got responsibilities—just like in high school when she labored at Nasty Burger to save some money for college. Unfortunately, getting ahead at many jobs requires a certain amount of playing after hours, something a mommy can no longer easily do. It's easy to feel a little left out, or left behind.

Since no one has invented a good solution to this problem, the same strategies that applied in high school apply at work. Excel in the hours you are there, always keeping the big picture and bigger prize in mind. Someday you'll own this place—or you'll win the lottery. If either happens, you'll be in a position to not give a damn about petty office politics. If that's too abstract for you, maintain the conviction that the really cute cheerleader and football player–types will eventually wind up dumpy and frumpy with their best days behind them. Perhaps it's not the most mature form of solace, but it is cheap, easy, and possibly the closest thing to satisfaction that the working Misfit Mom is likely to find.

Returning to work presents more than just philosophical challenges. There are plenty of logistical hurdles, too, and one of the biggest faced by new mommies is continuing to nurse while working full-time. The luckiest moms have on-site daycare and can nurse their infant whenever necessary. But most of us aren't that lucky—and that's where pumping comes in. Successful pumping requires time, privacy, and access to refrigeration. Most workplaces can come up with a refrigerator, but balk a little at the other two. Time is a major issue for many nursing moms. Although it doesn't take long to pump, some employers resent any time spent away from the job—the worst even dole out bathroom breaks like power-crazed elementary school hall monitors.

That some managers treat adults like truant children is maddening, but not uncommon. Many women in production and manufacturing jobs tell me that their every minute is counted, and their wages are docked if they take what are perceived as excessive breaks. As for privacy, it is increasingly rare in today's world of cubicles and communal workstations. Finding a quiet, private place to pump is a real challenge in many workplaces. I've talked to women who've pumped in bathroom stalls, broom closets, and storage rooms. I've also heard from employees at very forward-thinking companies who were provided with fully equipped lactation rooms, complete with comfortable seating, running water, and refrigeration. I'm guessing that most of us fall somewhere in the middle between a cramped seat on a bucket next to a hot water heater, and a recliner with a view of downtown. In whatever circumstances the Misfit Mom finds herself, she'll call on her considerable resources and generally make the best of it. That's what Misfits do. Along the way she'll also experience a new kind of empathy. Not just for other nursing moms, but for every prize-winning cow ever sponsored by 4-H.

Pumping looks and feels a little silly. How else to describe an activity that involves harnessing your breasts to a pair of suction cups attached to bottles, flipping a switch, and becoming a one-woman dairy barn? Pumping is neither painful nor difficult, but it is the sort of personal activity you'd rather not have interrupted by a surprise visit from a coworker. (Although that would give everyone involved a memory to last a lifetime.) Pumping is a little bit of a mind game, calling for the mother to relax enough to permit her milk to let down—without the usual feeding cues, i.e., a hungry baby wailing and rooting at your chest. There are a number of different things you can try to make it a bit easier. Some mothers look at a photograph of their baby; others dim the lights and try to recreate a nursing session in their minds. I asked dozens of nursing mothers to share their strategies. The most common answer was, "I wanted to nurse, which meant I had to pump. I just did it." Not coincidentally, the "just do it" moms were all Misfits, well experienced in the necessity of forging ahead no matter the obstacles.

One way to guarantee an easier time of it is to purchase or rent an electric double pump. It's fast, easy, and requires only that you hold the bottles steady while the machine does all the work. There are manual pumps on the market that are fine, but they are slower and more labor intensive. I also recall reading in one of the countless pregnancy books I purchased that breast milk could be hand-expressed into a sterile cup. Hmm. Sounds like a pleasant, efficient procedure, and a real timesaver—if you happen to believe that technology is inherently evil. Although all mothers should trust their instincts to guide their choices, milking oneself into a cup seems an extreme length to go for all but the most fanatical earth mother types. For those of us who choose not to live up in the trees, an electric breast pump is a great investment. Many hospitals also rent them but be warned: These rental units may not be the smallest or most lightweight options available. Get your gear-loving man involved in this particular decision. There are several good breast pumps on the market and he'll feel extra useful as he studies the various merits of each. Machinery, motors, and boobs—what guy wouldn't love that combination?

Pumped milk must be sealed in clean bottles or collection bags and refrigerated or frozen until ready for use. For most of us that means storing our milk in a communal refrigerator. People react to the presence of human milk in their fridge in a variety of ways: disgust, squeamishness, curiosity, irritation, or even horror. It's funny how many breast-obsessed adult Americans are absolutely appalled by sight of breast milk. Expect a certain amount of nervous joking and open revulsion. Why? Because many otherwise mature, rational adults display a kind of weird, childish prudery on the subject of human lactation. It is unlikely that you will succeed in helping these people overcome their discomfort, Misfit Mom, so drop the crusade. That we live in a world where the milk of dirty, cud-chewing, hooved bovines occupies a place of honor on our tables while nursing mothers frantically try to conceal all evidence of lactation, including hiding the finished product in tacky vinyl bags as though it were kryptonite in Superman's kitchen, is a sorry situation that one hopes time and education will alter. Anyone who considers it disgusting for their bologna sandwich to share refrigerator shelf space with your stored breast milk is not only an idiot unworthy of your greatly reduced time and energy, but obviously clueless as to the composition of bologna. As a busy working mommy, it's critical that you learn to choose your battles. This doesn't need to be one of them.

There's another battle you can opt out of, and it's a big one. It's the battle of rules, regulations, and "right" ways. The instant that babies became a billion-dollar business, the market was flooded with heaps of necessary items, essential gadgets, and reams and reams of instruction. This kind of tub, that kind of play yard (they were called "pens" when we were imprisoned in them, remember?), this bib, that mobile, a particular nightlight, a special this, that, and the other until a new mommy can't figure out what to wind up when.

Babies don't need or want a whole lot of stuff, but they do require, in addition to lots of love and gentle handling, set rituals and routines. Those routines don't have to come from a book or store. They can and should develop naturally from your life, and *your* or *your own family's* routines. For example, many working mommies come home utterly exhausted and launch immediately into feeding, bathing, and tending to their infant. Ragged, and without a moment to call their own, they cry, "I don't even have time to eat or take a shower!" It's easy to lose sight of the fact that motherhood is far more than an endless series of tasks and chores when you're facing . . . an endless series of tasks and chores.

With every new gadget and every new bit of expert advice, we've become a little more rigid in how we deal with our children to the point that we're afraid to improvise. Babies are durable, adventurous little souls. They'll happily comply with whatever routine we establish, even if it's a bit unorthodox. They don't know whether you're ferberizing, gerberizing, or schmerberizing them—and they don't care. Babies are great teachers in the subject of going with the flow. When my daughter was about a month old, I began taking her into the shower with me. Our shower stall was big enough for two, so I'd fill her little infant tub with warm water, nestle her into it, then shower while I bathed her. I was able to keep her out of the spray, yet nice and warm in the steamy enclosure. As she grew older, she'd kick her feet and giggle and play with a toy duck or a washcloth. Eventually she

Hop, Mommy!

Don't you wish you knew what your baby is thinking? I bet you can't wait for the day when your little bundle is able to communicate with words. You're imagining a sweet, chirping voice saying precious things like, "Hi, Mommy!" and "You're my mommy!" And, "I love you, Mommy!" You can expect babbling to turn into simple words like "mama" and "dada" by month nine. By eighteen months of age, your baby should be using simple two- or three-word sentences. Babies can also understand far more words than they are able to speak, so you can have reasonably sophisticated conversations with them, even though the only response they may be capable of contributing is "Yum juice!" What you're probably unprepared for is how swiftly your baby will learn to use his or her newly acquired language skills for the purpose of debate. "No" is a favorite first word for babies, one whose meaning they figure out very, very early. By twenty-three months, Olivia's vocabulary consisted mainly of commands. For example, in order to have her daddy all to herself for a bedtime story, Olivia would announce, "Night night, Mommy!"—while waving me toward the door. If that failed to banish me, she'd turn up the heat with a peremptory, "Away, Mommy!", also accompanied by a firm gesture of her miniature arm. When she'd had quite enough of a meal, or decided that a particular food was loathsome and unacceptable, she'd pick up her plate and hand it to us with a dismissive "Away!" I imagine that servants in royal households are made to endure similar treatment. Whether bellowing, "Ham! More ham!", or demanding that we draw, jump, hop, go, sit, ride, eat, or read a book, Olivia learned to talk by telling us what to do. And the drama if we failed to follow orders! She'd transform herself into a piteous, sobbing wretch, wailing, "Pink milk please!" or "Baby stein! Baby stein!" ("Stein" is Olivia shorthand for the *Baby Einstein* video series, which is, incidentally, the best friend a new parent could ever have. Purchase the entire set immediately.) Frustrating and confusing as an infant's cries can be, believe me when I tell you that a sixteen-month-old repeatedly shrieking the word "cookie" isn't a whole lot easier to deal with. At least with an infant you have the comfort of thinking that a good cuddle from you is the answer. An older baby will sell you out in a heartbeat for a graham cracker.

outgrew the tub and took to sitting on the floor surrounded by bath toys, splashing and happy. By eighteen months, she was standing under the water to be soaped and rinsed, clapping her hands as the bubbles swirled around her feet and down the drain.

Shower time is still one of our favorite activities, although now she tends to hog the water while forcing me to shampoo her doll's plastic head over and over again. Bathing for us became a joyful, shared activity that ended with lots of cuddles and clean pajamas for everyone. Not realizing what radical lunacy bathing with one's child apparently was, I casually mentioned it on the air. The collective response was outraged concern for my sanity. A baby in the shower! It's so slippery! You could drop her! Yes, and a dozen other awful but unlikely things could have happened too, and didn't. A baby in a tiny tub in the shower is no more hazardous than a baby in a tiny tub in the kitchen sink. As long as there is a sober mommy or daddy present, then it's simply another way to have a bath—not right or wrong, merely different.

A mommy who must divide her time between work and home needs flexibility not just in her schedule, but also in her thinking. For example, what is an appropriate bedtime? For a mommy who has been away from her baby all day, a seven or eight P.M. tuck-in may not provide enough time together. One mother I know resolved that dilemma by simply chucking the rules and doing what worked for her family. A night owl herself, she came to realize that the frustrating bedtime battle she and her husband faced each night with their infant son might be the product of trying to force a wakeful baby into a schedule that didn't fit him. By delaying her son's bedtime two hours, they had more family time—happy, pleasant family time—and much less resistance at bedtime. Do people think she's crazy for allowing an infant to stay up till ten? Yes. Does she care? Not a bit. She's enjoying her child with far less stress and fewer tears than before. And guess what? Your baby's bedtime is no one's business but your own. So what if people think you're nuts—like that's something new?

Using your judgment, taking the necessary safety precautions, and, most importantly, trusting your instincts allows you to care for your baby in your way. That's the beauty of being a mommy. You don't have to be an expert when it comes to all children, just your own. Working mommies who cultivate this confidence are more easily able to relax and take pleasure in their babies, while feeling less pressure on their already limited time. You might as well accept that there are no extra points awarded to mommies who insist on being saints or martyrs for their children. The only right way to parent is the one that works for you and your child—even if it runs counter to what friends, neighbors, or relatives advise.

As a mommy who must travel for business, I dreaded leaving my baby behind. As a nursing mommy, I refused to. That meant hauling Olivia from one end of the country to the other for the first year of her life. My husband's decision to walk away from his engineering career to stay home with our daughter made this possible. We traveled together as a family, which added up to all sorts of adventures, and allowed us to be together as much as possible. With the full support of my company, a rare and lucky thing for a working mommy, I was able to balance job and baby with minimal disruption. It's amazing what's possible when working mothers are treated as assets instead of liabilities.

Syndicated radio can be great fun, but it's not always glamorous. Sure, there were trips to Sonoma County and Hilton Head Island, but our specialty ran more to towns that don't get profiled in glossy travel magazines. With baby in tow, we traveled to Wisconsin, Georgia, upstate New York, Florida, California, and Kentucky. By six months of age, Olivia was a seasoned flyer and an old hand at navigating hotels. However, babies grow up and with every day she became more independent and less interested in being strapped into her car seat for another airplane ride. Newborn babies function a little like carry-on luggage; older babies are more like rambunctious wild animals—the kind that never do well in cages. When I received an invitation to speak on a panel at an industry convention, I decided with a heavy heart that perhaps this should be thirteen-month-old Olivia's last cross-country business trip.

This particular *Radio & Records* convention was held at the Beverly Hilton in Beverly Hills—a pretty swanky setting for a less than swanky industry. The fun thing about attending an *R&R* convention is the people. Grab a drink and a seat in the lobby of any *R&R* hotel, any city, any year, and you'll see a show. People in the record business and their radio brethren are so determined to be original and non-conformist that everyone shows up looking exactly like everyone else. The slightly older guys who deal mostly with money wear black t-shirts under sport jackets, with jeans or black pants. The younger guys who deal mostly with kissing the butts of the older guys wear a hybrid skater/surfer/disaffected alt-rock look complete with multiple piercings, tattoos, and hair colors. The relatively few women resemble guitar players in all-girl garage bands, or the blowsy but still sexy managers of local rock bars. That so many individuals trying so hard to be different could somehow manage to come together and collectively generate the wretched corporate sameness that is commercial radio is a wonder—but it's not a riddle that anyone attending an *R&R* is likely to solve. The biggest excitement is reserved for the hospitality suites (free booze), the guest artists (big-name acts with records to sell), and the parties (one year the hot ticket was the Playboy Mansion—mecca to the typical radio geek). Needless to say, there were never any babies in attendance.

Olivia was unimpressed by the scene at the Beverly Hilton. Either she was too young to schmooze, or too addled by the time change to notice her surroundings. That is, she would have been addled by the time change if she'd paid any attention to it. One of the things that no one ever mentions about traveling with an infant is their complete disinterest in playing the time zone game. Olivia was an eastern baby everywhere she went. She awoke every morning promptly at 7:00, which meant that she was wide-awake and ready to rumble at 4:00 A.M. Los Angeles time. Bleary and tongue-tied from exhaustion, I offered my husband anything he wanted—anything—to just please take her out of the room and let me sleep for another hour. My groveling worked, and off they went into predawn Beverly Hills.

Two and a half hours later I opened my eyes to a beaming baby and a cup of coffee. My husband reported that they'd gone for a long walk through the neighborhood and up Rodeo Drive. I asked if he'd spotted any stars. He snorted. "Stars? You're kidding, right? Nobody's out in Beverly Hills this time of day but winos—and me. I was the only guy on Wilshire pushing a baby carriage that had an actual baby in it. You're on your own for the next convention. We're never doing this again." And so ended the glorious era of traveling everywhere with my baby.

That it started on a golf course in Wisconsin and ended in Beverly Hills seemed an apt enough metaphor for this mommy's lower tier showbiz career—but I didn't come away empty-handed. There are things you can do to help make travel easier for babies. Here are the ten most useful things I learned in a year of heavy-duty baby travel:

1. When possible, schedule your flight to coincide with a feeding—or adjust your feeding schedule to fit your takeoff time. Wait to start nursing or feeding until the plane is ready to taxi. This will accomplish two things. First, the act of swallowing during takeoff will help equalize the pressure in baby's ears; after all, you can't very well expect the tiny thing to chew a stick of gum, can you? Second, a full baby very often becomes a sleepy baby. Napping makes the flight go by faster for everyone. I shared this bit of advice with a new mommy on her way to Texas. Her baby had already sobbed his way across the U.S. once, and she was dreading the return. She called me later to tell me it had worked like a charm—and that she couldn't believe she hadn't thought of it on her own. Maybe she would have had she not been so hesitant to try anything with her child that she hadn't first read in a book. See what I mean about our being afraid to improvise?

2. The airlines won't require you to buy a seat for a child under age two, but if it's a long flight and if you can at all afford it, buy one anyway. An infant strapped into a car seat

that's been buckled into an airplane seat is safer, more comfortable, and more likely to sleep than an infant perched on the few inches of your lap that the standard seat in coach provides. No mommy wants to see her wee precious launched airborne in a bout of severe turbulence, right? Buying a seat also saves you the hassle of gate-checking your car seat. Before the airlines tightened their security and baggage rules, it seemed like only parents were singled out for gate checking, while their fellow passengers merrily stuffed fresh sides of beef and pinball machines into the overhead bins. Childless fliers who've never had to gate-check anything will have at least observed the tired, ashen, hollow-eyed creatures who inexplicably stand in the jetway after disembarking, as though reluctant to exchange the clouds for the painfully earthbound airport terminal that awaits. Those are not lost souls but simply parents who've gate-checked car seats and strollers.

3. If you do buy an airline seat for your baby, be sure to indicate that your fellow passenger is an infant. That's often worth a sizable discount. But beware: The airlines like to stuff families traveling with children into the back of the plane, close to the lavatory. That may be nirvana for the mommy whose bladder didn't get the memo about how helpful all those Kegel exercises were supposed to be, but it's a nightmare for anyone prone to airsickness. If you find yourself assigned to steerage and call to change your seats only to be told that the plane is fully booked, there is one thing you can still do to circumvent this treachery. Wait until twenty-four to thirty hours prior to your flight. The airlines often release seats at that time, and you can easily

make changes to your reservation online, without having to sit in a telephone queue or talk to a living soul. We've successfully done this a number of times, including on flights to Jackson, Wyoming—a destination always choked with planeloads of investment bankers dressed up in their version of authentic ski and cowboy wear. It's nice to let them get a taste of reality in the last row while we sit up front and chuckle into our apple juice.

4. If you think you can beat the system by leaving your car seat at home and renting one from a car rental agency, think again. Their definition of an infant safety seat may be very different from yours. Bear in mind that no amount of conversation on the phone with a reservations agent will provide any real information with which to make your decision. Here's an example of what I mean: After being reassured that the seat we were renting was in fact meant for an infant, we showed up in Salt Lake City to claim our car and seat—only to be handed a grubby and battered booster seat intended for a child of about four. (By "grubby" I mean filthy to the point that we were hesitant to touch it with our bare hands.) Our questions and gentle protests were greeted with an implacable, "That's-the-only-kind-we-have-next-please." And that's how we found ourselves, half an hour later, purchasing a brand-new infant car seat at a K-Mart in Park City, Utah. Babies cannot travel safely in booster seats, and it's against both the law and common sense to drive with your baby rolling around loose in the car. While I'm sure that it's possible to successfully rent an infant seat along with an automobile, I don't recommend that any mommy make herself the guinea pig in that experiment.

Why risk any additional aggravation in an already stressful situation? You cannot even begin to imagine how safety obsessed you'll be as a new mommy. In the long run, it's much easier on you and your sanity to simply travel with your own car seat.

5. In the interest of fairness, we cut a pretty wide swath through the hospitality industry, from the Ritz-Carlton to a roadside motel so unsavory that we were frightened to remove our shoes. In every instance we found staff happy to accommodate an infant. Unless you're staying at the sort of hotel where rooms are rented by the hour, you *won't* need to bring a portable crib with you on the road. Do make sure to request a crib when you reserve your room, though, since many hotels keep only a few on hand. What you should pack is your own baby bedding. Not because the hotel won't supply you with something, but because you never know what that something will be. I've seen everything from a proper crib sheet and matching bumpers to a full-size hotel sheet folded to fit. A fitted sheet and blanket won't take up much space in your bag, and it's easier to go ahead and bring your own than to worry about your baby smothering in too much bedding.

6. If you plan to share a single room with baby for more than a couple of nights, whether in a hotel or at your in-laws, you might want to invest in a small white-noise generator, sometimes called a *sleep machine*. These devices, which generally retail for thirty to fifty dollars, create a soothing hum that helps mask other, more distracting noise—like conversation, or traffic. Using the sleep machine while baby naps can make it possible for you to move around the room, or

for other members of the household to go about their business without fear of waking the wee beast. Restless babies unused to sharing a room with mommy and daddy may also be extra wakeful due to hearing your breathing and movements in the night. By helping to mask those sounds, a sleep machine can make the difference between actually sleeping at night, versus spending the night trying to get your baby to sleep.

7. When traveling with an infant, room service isn't an indulgence or a rip-off; it's a godsend. Why drag a weary, fussy baby into a restaurant when you can bring the restaurant right to your room? Baby can snooze or have a little tummy time with a favorite toy on a blanket on the floor while you relax and actually enjoy a meal. This is definitely one of those instances where the aggravation you'll save is well worth the extra money you'll spend. Hotels will happily supply kettles of hot water and clean bowls so that you can prepare cereal and, best of all, no one will give you a dirty look if your baby screams, cries, or barfs.

8. Disposable diapers are bulky, heavy, and take up way too much space in a suitcase. If you're planning to be gone for more than a weekend, travel only with what you need for the journey, then buy the rest when you arrive at your destination. Going to visit family or friends? Let them be as helpful as they claim they want to be by sending them out to buy diapers before you arrive. Ditto for wipes and baby food. I promise that diapers and pureed squash are sold in all but the most remote outposts. You're a mommy, not a pack mule.

9. Although traveling by car with a young baby is relatively

easy (it does get harder, and that's a promise), even they get
bored and irritable, and can suffer from "seat fatigue."
There's nothing more distracting or distressing than trying
to drive with an infant's high-decibel wailing in your ears.
Time your car trip so that you can depart at naptime. That
way you'll start your journey in relative peace, and will
have a shot at making some real progress before it's time to
stop. And you *will* have to stop, not just for feeding and diapers, but also for cuddling and play. Sometimes all it takes to
calm a raging road baby is twenty minutes outside the car.
Get off the highway, head into a little town or rest area, and
take a walk. Everyone will feel calmer and more ready to
continue. As much of a hurry as we're all perpetually in, it
really is better to arrive an hour late and sane, than right on
time and completely out of your mind.

10. Never go *anywhere* without some sort of stroller. Collapsible
or *umbrella* strollers can be had for about twenty dollars, and
it's one purchase you won't regret. Babies are just like
people—albeit very small and unreasonable ones—when it
comes to travel. New surroundings, a disrupted schedule,
and a strange bed can all add up to fussiness and insomnia.
There's nothing like a walk to soothe a peevish baby. In our
year of serious baby travel, my husband logged countless
miles of stroller pushing—from Lexington, Kentucky, to the
streets of Manhattan, all the way to Malibu and back again.
You may curse the stroller while you're trying to shove it
into the overpacked trunk of your car or while you're waiting for it to be unloaded from the plane, but you'll ultimately thank it for saving you from many long nights with
an overtired, inconsolable baby. Not to mention the fact that

traveling with a baby involves carrying loads of extra gear.
You'll be glad for a stroller to take some of that weight.

Returning to work, to the sometimes tedious, sometimes wonderful
routines that make up our daily lives is a challenge, but it's one we can
handle. By breaking a big, intimidating undertaking down into separate, manageable tasks and always asking not just "What is good for
baby?" but also "What works best for me?", mommies can fulfill their
obligations without becoming ragged martyrs. With all the planning,
and strategizing, and maneuvering of necessary goods and objects
from place to place, motherhood can feel a bit like a military exercise.
That gives the Misfit Mom a real edge when it comes to mastering the
basics. Think of it this way: Every new day brings with it a new
opportunity for the Misfit Mom to accomplish a new goal. That's very
satisfying for the achievement-oriented Misfit Mom. From feeding and
diapering, to making the working mommy choice actually work for
you, this is a chance for the Misfit to shine, to feel capable and confident and strong.

Return to work with a steely new resolve. Having a baby hasn't
diminished you—just the opposite. You are all you ever were, and
more. Once you've had a baby, what middle management weasel can
faze you? Let them drone on and on about how there's no *I* in team and
all of that faux-psychology hot air that's meant to be motivating but
instead drives intelligent people bats. You've just manufactured an
entire human being inside your body, pushed it into the world despite
mind-altering pain, and are now feeding, nurturing, and watching it
grow. You are brave, capable, resilient, and beautiful. You are a *warrior*.
And you're getting all the smiles and approval you need at home. Step
aside, puny beings! Be silent, blithering fools! *Mommy is on the job.*

11

Hello, My Name Is Mommy

One of the hardest things for new mommies to master is the art of perspective. It's easy to forget that your screaming, colicky baby, the one who's kept you awake for almost thirty-two hours straight, the one who won't eat, sleep, or be consoled, the one who is causing you to suffer from fatigue so profound that you are now hallucinating and barely coherent, will not be a baby forever. In fact, said baby will be walking, talking, and asking you for money before you know it. The months spent caring for your infant are consuming and exhausting, but when you look at your life as a whole, relatively brief. Remembering this is key to harnessing your mommy power. Your worst day as a new mommy is just that—a day. A minute of misery can't last any longer than a minute of joy, although it's a fact that one minute with a shrieking six-month-old actually does feel like eternity.

When things aren't going well, and sometimes they won't despite all of your best efforts and preparation, self-doubt swiftly moves in to wallop a new mommy. Little challenges with a baby have a way of magnifying themselves into enormous difficulties. When you're crazy-tired and feeling overwhelmed by new responsibilities, it's easy to let emotion overtake reason. Every single thing that your baby does—or doesn't do—becomes weighted with consequence. A day or two of disinterest in eating morphs into potential starvation. A tummyache might very well be a bowel obstruction. Slow progress in rolling over or sitting up starts to look suspiciously like a developmental delay. Infants can't talk, leaving their mommies to interpret every grimace, grunt, squeal, and squeak. Prone to rehearsing catastrophe anyway, the Misfit Mom almost can't help herself from projecting all sorts of melodramatic scenarios onto her helpless baby. This is why perspective is so critical. Without it, parents go crazy, and crazy parents are what got us all into this mess, right?

The first step in gaining perspective comes when we acknowledge that there is no such thing as a perfect family or a perfect mommy. Those are fairy tale creations, the stuff of storybooks and television shows. Misfits would seem unlikely candidates for belief in such fantasy, but just the opposite is true. Having spent years yearning for the ideal family and investing it with almost supernatural powers for good, Misfits are true believers in the family as an heroic institution. We enter adulthood with plenty of ideas about the kinds of families we hope to create for ourselves. Those ideas, some very good, others completely unrealistic, can get us into all sorts of well-intentioned trouble. The Misfit Mom intent on building the perfect family can be swiftly derailed by the normal, day-to-day mess and conflict that spouses and children will routinely throw at her. When the Misfit Mom has a family agenda and others don't cooperate with her script, look out. Either it's perfectionist control-freak time, or a pity party for She Who Can Do Nothing Right.

If ever a fantasy needed a bucket of cold water chucked on it, it's the glowing image of all-competent, all-knowing, self-sacrificing motherhood. Real women cannot live up to these near-mythic standards, and it's a crying shame that so many of us measure our worth as mothers largely by the degree to which we fall short of this ideal. How can you ever hope to enjoy your children, or the experience of mothering them, if what you're really focused on is critiquing your own performance and keeping score?

If you're wearing yourself out to keep Little Precious in designer rompers while simultaneously growing your own organic peas and carrots in the misguided hope that everyone will notice what a spectacular mommy you are, wake up. No one is paying any attention to your bid for martyrdom. Everyone you are secretly hoping to impress is too busy dealing with the drama of their own lives to be awestruck spectators at yours. So relax, sponge the spit-up off the baby, and order a pizza. And repeat after me: There is no such thing as a perfect mommy. I will *not* be the exception to this rule. Even if I try really, really hard.

The second step in gaining perspective is to relinquish control over every single event that transpires in your household or with your child. This is easier said than done. I got a fortune cookie once that read, "Hands clenched tightly are not open to receive treasure." It's the perfect bit of wisdom for control freaks to live by, even if it did arrive wadded up inside a pastry. Unfortunately, years of childlessness have given the Misfit Mom a false sense of mastery over her domain. Things stay where you put them, machinery functions as it ought to, and supplies flow in and out of your life in a fairly predictable manner. All of this will change with the arrival of a baby. Babies gum up the works. Oh, not permanently, but enough to drive you mad in the short term. For a period ranging from three months to two years, you will experience shortages (toilet paper, artificial sweetener, television remotes, stamps); power outages (broken washing machine, dishwasher, furnace, a/c unit); and riots (missing binkies, loathsome pureed foods, husband wanting sex). Throw up your hands now and surrender. The philosophy: She who refuses to enter the battle cannot be defeated.

Although the closest most Misfits ever get to the concept of Zen is when we jot it on a to-do list then forget to do anything about it, the Zen approach may be the healthiest a new mommy can take. In a much-simplified nutshell: The Buddha realized that all of life is subject to change, and that suffering and unhappiness are rooted in our attachment to things that are not permanent. Letting go of those attachments frees us from suffering. All, and I do mean all, of the strife that a newborn brings into your life falls into this impermanent category. Baby refusing vegetables? Toilet backing up? Boss yammering on about some trifle or another? All temporary. Let go of the need to control—your attachment, in other words—sit back, and take a few deep breaths. Have a latte. This is not giving up or laziness. This is enlightenment. You'll be a better mommy—and a happier one, too. You spent months *looking* like the Buddha; now it's time to start thinking like him, too. Repeat after me: I am relinquishing control. Control breeds suffering. All is subject to change, although not necessarily because I demand it, even when I am clearly in the right.

The third and final step in gaining perspective involves taking a long, loving look at the most resourceful and reliable person you have ever known: yourself. Ten years of talking to women about their lives has taught me that most of us have no idea how strong and beautiful and amazing we are. Where we should see grace and power, we see fat thighs, crow's feet, and flabby tummies. Where we ought to celebrate tenacity and courage, we instead point out fear and insecurity. Where we should draw the line, we take the blame. We apologize too much and demand too little. Many Misfit Moms are clever, capable survivors who haven't yet realized that the war is over—and we've won. We're here. That's what matters. There's nothing else to prove. The only thing truly skewed or distorted about you is your own self-image.

The Misfit who sees herself through the same coldly critical eyes that have been calculating the odds stacked against her since she was a little girl is always going to see someone ugly and flawed who doesn't belong. That those eyes are her own makes it all the more difficult to escape their scrutiny. Don't believe it? Just for fun, go dig out the pictures you took for your Home Soft Core Photo Shoot (see chapter four). Before you look at them, take a moment to remember exactly how you felt about your body at the time those photos were taken. Let's run through the standard adjectives of Misfit self-loathing: dumpy, flabby, soft, doughy, lumpy, spongy, pasty, hairy, gross, repulsive, and disgusting. Insert your own if I've left out a personal favorite. All set? Now look at the pictures. Remarkable. The prebaby you was pretty hot, wasn't she? She's curvy and healthy, and so much prettier than you remember. Perhaps you're thinking, "Why didn't I

Think You're Tired Now?

There's nothing like reading aloud to spark your baby's imagination and budding intellect. It's one of the single most important things a parent can do. Babies love repetition, and rarely tire of hearing their favorite stories over and over. In fact, you'll spend so much time chanting Dr. Seuss at your little wide-eyed future genius that, after a while, even your thoughts will take on the loopy meter of *The Cat in the Hat*:

Take a nap!
Take a nap!
Take a nap PLEASE!

You can't spend all day
Lounging here on my knees!
There are messes to clean,
Spills to mop up!
Like the milk that you launched straight out of your cup!
And those crayons! What happened?
You flushed the whole box?
What's that floating with them—
Are those Daddy's socks?
Oh the chaos! The mayhem!
The fuss and the muddle!
And you all serene
Sitting smack in a puddle!
Of something or other that's all wet and sticky,
And bound to be gross and most certainly icky!
It's amazing how much you can do with no sleep!
The things you accomplish! The hurdles you leap!
I can juggle the dishes and answer the door,
And talk on the phone while I vacuum the floor.
And moo like a cow and play "This Little Piggy,"
And listen to Barney without going wiggy.
I can even make dinner from canned peas and salami—
When did it happen?
I've turned into a mommy!

know how good I looked then?" If you can manage to add, "And as tired and flabby and hideous as I feel now, maybe I still look pretty good," then congratulations. That's not just perspective; it's an epiphany. Too bad you can't take a snapshot of your heart or soul in the same way. If you could, you'd marvel to discover so much grace and bravery, compassion and decency, and a readiness to love without boundaries. You'd want to be just like you.

For the Misfit Mom seeking exactly the right path, it may be little consolation to realize that no one has a map anymore. There are as many different ways to be a mommy as there are mommies to invent them. Motherhood is not a competition, though some moms work overtime to make it one, piling activities, enrichments, and products onto babies not old enough to have properly discovered their own feet. Nor is motherhood a minefield of potential tragedy, just waiting to snare the offspring of the woman thoughtless enough to have sneaked into the bathroom for five selfish minutes alone. Perspective is invaluable. It's the basis of Mom Power.

Take any serene, calm, competent mother you have ever known or observed. What do these apparently unflappable goddesses have in common? They know the difference between an actual crisis and a trivial event. Crisis: Child needs stitches. Trivial event: Child needs Band-Aid. Crisis: Child eats dog's flea collar. Trivial event: Dog eats child's Teletubby figurine. Reacting to every trivial event as though it were a five-alarm fire is exhausting and counterproductive for a mommy, and worse, may result in your child sharing that same overwrought inability to cope. A boo-boo is not the same as a gunshot, and a spilled cup of juice is not equivalent to an earthquake. If you don't see blood or flames, calm down. If you don't require emergency vehicles or help from poison control, calm down. In fact, if you can resolve your crisis with a kiss, a PowerPuff Band-Aid, an orange Popsicle, or a roll of paper towels, then whatever it is can't be all that bad, can it?

Perspective is power. You won't have it at the beginning, not when every yip or yowl emitted by your newborn will whip the entire household into a frenzy of trying to determine exactly what it is that the baby needs. Perspective comes with experience, and from trusting in your own good sense. That should give the Misfit an edge—and she'll need it. A day comes for all of us when even the most high-performing Misfit Mom has to face the fact that she's only human—and a weary, overextended human at that. Maybe that moment will come for you on the day that your baby is teething and won't stop fussing long enough to sleep, the hot water heater springs a leak, the dog wanders in with a sudden and mysterious swelling over his eye, and your husband gets violently ill from a fast-food taco. Meanwhile, you've rushed off to an important meeting at work, where you're busy trying to discreetly pick Cheerios out of your bra. Days like that are coming. Many of them. There are basically two ways to react: fall apart and blame yourself for being unable to cope, turning your household upside down as you rage and/or wail like a unstable harridan. This is the strategy to adopt if you're aiming to frighten the baby and freak out your husband. Or, pour a glass of wine, shove the junk mail and Clifford books to the side of the table, and start making yet another to-do list. This is the strategy to adopt if you'd like to maintain a shred of dignity under duress. At least this time the chaos all around you is no one's fault. It's just life with a baby, and even the most compulsive Misfit will never be able to control it, corral it, or contain it.

The following things are going to start happening to you on a fairly regular basis. They will defy your rule and test your patience, stamina, and self-esteem. These things happen to every parent. You are not being singled out, nor are you the victim of your own stupidity, inadequacy, or poor upbringing. Normal women have these same tribulations—they just don't assume that all of it is their fault. (That's one of the major fringe benefits of being normal—such people are actually able to blame something other than themselves for mishaps, mistakes, and mayhem. Imagine that.)

Your house will be a mess.

Toys will be strewn everywhere.

You will find crayons in your shoes, and half-chewed bagels in
your purse.

Your baby will get sick, even if he never leaves the house.

Your baby will wipe her nose on the shoulder of your freshly
dry-cleaned blouse.

Your baby will fall and bang her head.

Your baby will trip and scrape his face.

Your baby will throw up, often on you.

You will discuss—and dwell upon—every aspect of your
child's bowel movements.

Ear infections will always announce themselves at three A.M.

There will always be laundry waiting to be folded.

Babysitters cancel.

Your baby will draw on the walls.

Your baby will use the cuticle scissors to give himself a Three
Stooges haircut.

You will have no idea how the baby got scissors. Ditto for
Magic Markers.

Withered objects that turn out to be half-chewed raisins will
start appearing everywhere.

Apple juice will be spilled.

Milk will be spilled.

Soup will be spilled.

Your baby will push you away and scream for daddy.

Mysterious stains will appear on your clothes.

Baby will wander off with your keys/phone/remote/watch.

You will not be able to remember names or dates.

You will be too tired for sex.

You will be too tired to think.

You will sometimes feel like the most inept, incompetent mother
  alive.

You will be weary and frustrated enough to cry.

Nobody ever said it was easy to be a mommy, though it certainly
doesn't *look* all that hard to the uninitiated. Catch a mommy on a good
day when baby is content to quietly look adorable in Osh Kosh over-
alls while mommy shops, eats, or holds up her end of the conversation,
and you can't be blamed for thinking, "What's all the fuss about?"
Catch her on a bad day and you'll end up swearing to never mother
anything more challenging than a puppy. When it comes to parenting,
the extreme difficulty of the job is precisely what makes it so rewarding. It's like all of life in that the hardest stuff always proves to be most
wonderful in the long run. If that weren't the case, true fulfillment
would come less from working hard and doing the right things and
more from lying on the couch and eating Oreos while watching endless repeats of *Sex and the City*.

   You can prepare for pregnancy. You can prepare for the first few
weeks with a newborn, though you will have to be abducted, held
behind enemy lines, and tortured with a variety of methods including
sleep deprivation, noise immersion, and starvation, to truly approxi-
mate the newborn experience. But you can never prepare for the reality of loving someone so much that your identity blurs and transforms.
When people say that motherhood will change you, they don't mean
that your hips will be wider or your fashion sense less savvy, or your
politics suddenly more conservative. In loving a child we taste our
own mortality, our very real fragility, and overnight we know what it
truly means to have something, everything, to lose.

   When we sign on for the job of mommy, we step into a role so well known and beloved that the whole audience can chant our lines. Mommies are superheroes minus the cape, movie stars minus the glamour, and angels minus the wings. Like firefighters, cowboys, and rock stars, mommies are larger than life. Even the littlest kids know the score: Firefighters are courageous; cowboys ride horses; rock stars are rich. And mommy? Mommy sacrifices herself to help the dreams of all the others come true. Motherhood is freighted with symbolism, mythology, hope, expectation, and so much lofty purpose that no mortal woman can ever possibly get it all right. Look at just some of the words that we associate with motherhood: selflessness, generosity, patience, wisdom, charity, purity, gentle, resourceful, agreeable, strength, thrifty, clean, serenity, peace, virtue, protective, cautious, tolerant. All worthy characteristics, not to mention a very high set of standards for any human being to aspire to.

Of course we want our mothers to be all of those things and more—and we dream of being that kind of mother ourselves. Yet here you are with a very small baby, staring at a very large learning curve, and wondering if maybe the mommy fairies forgot to sprinkle you with that magical motherhood dust before you left the hospital. If you don't feel like the mothers celebrated in greeting cards and sappy songs, congratulations: You're normal. No one feels like that, especially not at first. The kind of motherhood that seems most at home when perched on a pedestal takes years and years to achieve. We're entry level: all elbows and thumbs and big ideas. Our toolboxes may be empty, but we do have the one thing necessary to be a good mommy: the honest love in our heart for the child in our arms. Everything else has to be figured out along the way. It works that way for everyone.

Mommies are immersed in such a deafening chorus of *shoulds* and *shouldn't*s that it's a wonder we can even hear our babies, much less our own thoughts. The shoulds and shouldn'ts are the sometimes subtle, sometimes blatant messages that all women pick up their whole lives, and especially when we become mothers. Our own inner voice is often the loudest of all. *A good mommy should cook nutritious foods, keep a spotless house, do laundry. A good mommy should help with homework, be willing to play, volunteer where needed. A good mommy should be patient and slow to anger. A good mommy should be available, and should put her own needs last.* Likewise, a not-so-good mommy is just as easy to spot. *A mommy shouldn't expect much freedom, or go out often with friends. A mommy shouldn't let kids watch television, or rely on convenience foods. A mommy shouldn't spend money on herself, worry about her clothing, or drive an impractical car. A mommy shouldn't be too sexual, or work if she doesn't have to.* The reconciling of these many expectations, some good, some outdated, some completely unrealistic, makes motherhood the ultimate Misfit Mom challenge. Ever the perfectionist, she is a sitting duck for the shoulds and shouldn'ts, just waiting to have her flimsy defenses blown out of the sky.

What makes motherhood extra tricky is that it is a public job and, like it or not, every aspect of your life as a mother is up for debate. Complete strangers will feel perfectly comfortable weighing in on how you feed, clothe, discipline, and instruct your children. They'll unload a pile of shoulds and shouldn'ts on you so quick that your stroller wheels will spin. Believe it. And believe that you'll be vulnerable to words and ideas that would have made no sense at all prior to having a baby. That's because we all possess more ideas and expectations about motherhood and ourselves as mothers than we are even conscious of. Things sneak up that you never dreamed or envisioned, from feeling guilty over not being able to sew a dragon costume for a six-year-old, to yearning for the seemingly easier life of the past, when women had fewer choices, and thus fewer conflicts. The Misfit has all of the same sitcom-style, Hallmark card, pink and fuzzy mommy ideals as any other woman—but with an extra load of boxes marked "Shattered—may be inadequate."

Making peace with the past is no small feat for the Misfit Mom. The birth of a child, while tremendously healing, also brings up fresh pain and new realizations. Loving your own child can be a stark reminder that you were not so loved. Caring for, nurturing, and protecting your child may cast a harsh light on the lack of that same kind of care and nurture in your own childhood. Many of your parents' actions and choices will become even harder to understand once you become a parent yourself. Might as well prepare for that right now. Transforming parental abuse or abandonment into a comfortable abstraction is much easier to do before you cradle your own infant in your arms. Anger or grief that you didn't know you still felt may surface when you least expect it, leaving the Misfit Mom to despair of ever being able to put the past behind her.

Purge those dregs, speak those feelings aloud, even if to no one but yourself. Cry those tears, and think of them as a gift: You can still feel. Those places in your heart that you feared were dead were only numbed. Let being a mommy help you restore that part of yourself for good. But know that it takes time. It's far easier to preach forgiveness than it is to practice it. However, like it or not, there can be no lasting happiness or peace for you until you are able to forgive the past. Knock on a million doors—therapists, priests, gurus, mentors, shamans, any and every soul who claims to have the answers—but there's no escaping the truth that peace comes only through forgiveness. Forgiveness is not amnesia; there is no forgetting the pain and hurt you have suffered. Forgiveness is more like letting out a breath that's been held far too long. Until you do, nothing can ever be over and your past will always cast a shadow on your present. You deserve a better, richer life than that, a life that has so far eluded you. Knowing that your child needs a mommy unburdened by ghosts may be what you require to let go, to forgive and finally move on. It's worth the struggle, not just for our children, but for ourselves as well.

Having been denied a good bit of the magic of childhood when we were actually children, Misfit Moms have one major advantage working in our favor: There's a part of us, way deep down, that never stopped believing in it. Whether it's the Tooth Fairy or Santa, Misfit Moms love the trappings of childhood. Though we can never again be so unspoiled and innocent ourselves, we haven't forgotten the thrill of belief. Maybe that's because instead of being permitted to outgrow it naturally, we were wrenched away and thrust prematurely into adulthood. There's a part of us that's never finished growing up, that loves costumes and playacting, bubble gum machines and soap bubbles, that still wishes on birthday candles and stars. Hidden beneath layers of cynicism and worldliness and our shiny tough-girl veneer is a flicker of childhood, one that a Misfit Mom can yet fan into a flame. Those joys have not been lost forever. Parenthood restores the magic and wonder of childhood to us, and more, it makes us into wizards. Parents have the power to summon pure awe and wide-eyed astonishment. That power is yours now, and when you wave your wand the little girl inside you will clap her hands with every bit the same delight as the child who calls you mommy. You can, in a sense, grow up all over again, and this time there is nothing to fear.

Our lives are ultimately the stories we tell. The roles we are cast in, victim or villain, hero or martyr, princess or little girl lost, are not fixed in stone. We really do have the power to decide who we are, and, ultimately, who we will become. Hasn't the Misfit always known that? Hasn't she lived every day with that conviction? That faith is what enabled the Misfit to survive and thrive in a world where so many of the bets were laid against her. But the Misfit Mom who bets on herself will always come up a winner. Even when she screws up and loses her temper, her sanity, and her way—as every mommy sooner or later will—the Misfit knows how to pick herself up and keep moving, no matter how slow or steep the road becomes. The beautiful thing about being a Misfit Mommy is this: After what you've already endured, there is precious little that can throw you now. Bring on the spit up, the sleepless nights, the tantrums. Don't forget the whining and crying, the mess, the noise, and enough worry to last a lifetime. Just make sure you add the milky kisses, the tiny hands that squeeze your fingers tight, and the pleasantly solid, plump warmth of a very small body nestled against your own.

We have so few rituals that celebrate the uniquely female events in our lives. Unlike the Yanomami tribe of Brazil, we don't commemorate our first menstruation with a trip to a ceremonial hut deep in the forest. Having grown up on a steady television diet of maxi pads with wings, we tend to view our periods more as a nuisance than as a magical rite of passage. Unless you have a bat mitzvah, a confirmation, or a quinceaneara, chances are good that your transition from girl to woman won't be formally celebrated. Which is too bad, especially since we grow up hearing a lot of bad news about what it means to be a girl in our society. So much of the female experience has been cast in a negative light: we have "the curse." We get PMS. Pregnancy makes us fat or gives us stretch marks. Menopause makes us weepy or deranged or even asexual. And that's just the body's mischief; there's a world of other political, financial, and cultural hurdles laid out before us.

Invading extraterrestrials could be excused for mistaking feminin- ity for a disease, one causing chronic cramping, bloating, crying, hot flashes, weight gain, and inappropriate body hair. We hold ourselves to the impossible, air-brushed standards of our celebrity-addled age, then hate ourselves when we fail to measure up. Brains, guts, great ideas are all well and good, but you'd better look like a walking, talking shampoo ad if you really want to get ahead, right? It's tough to feel like a goddess when so much of your energy is wasted explaining, defending, and justifying. Why not seize the opportunity that motherhood offers to cut yourself loose from some of the expectations that bind you in self-doubt, even self-hatred? Motherhood is not merely a lifestyle choice. It's not just another excuse to go shopping. It is the rite of passage that transforms us into warriors.

Blood, pain, sacrifice—these have long been the elements of initiation into warrior status. Until it was outlawed in the 1800s, young Crow Indians who wished to become warriors were first required to participate in a ritual known as the Sun Dance. A tribal medicine man would take a fold of skin on the initiate's chest and skewer it with a length of bone. That bone would be attached with a piece of rope to a pole thrust into the ground. The young man then danced for hours, with the ritual culminating in his breaking free of the pole. To do so meant literally tearing and ripping open his own flesh. Survival proved more than courage; it demonstrated an ability to endure pain and extreme suffering—all self-inflicted. It was seen as a physical, emotional, and spiritual rebirth. Only then might a warrior be entrusted with the sacred duties of protecting and defending the tribe.

Change the scene: a clean, modern hospital room. Strip away the comforts of technology and what remains is one individual testing the limits of her strength and endurance, giving over her flesh to the miracle of new, raw human life. And it *is* your miracle. It doesn't matter how many millions and billions of other babies have been born on this planet. A miracle is made no less profound by repetition. Celebrate your own role in that miracle. Believe that like any true warrior, you have been tested and transformed. You are bigger, braver, and wiser than you ever knew. That's good, because amazing challenges lie ahead, along with the tears and laughter, the joys and perils of deep and unconditional commitment. You're prepared for all of it, no matter what sorrows haunt your past. The dance is just beginning.

To become a mother is to be more loved, more needed, and more alive than you've ever felt. Every drooling embrace, every toothless smile, every burbled utterance of your name is a reminder that you are *mommy*, the most wonderful and important and beloved person on earth. Your touch is the most craved, your arms are the most comforting, and your voice is the sweetest of all possible sounds. To become a mommy is to be offered another chance, an opportunity at a life truly lived, not merely survived. To become a mommy is to see not just your world but your capacity for faith and wonder enlarged. You are part of a special sisterhood now, an unbroken chain of mothers that stretches all the way back to the dimmest reaches of time. A good mommy is not simply born and can never be bought, but instead is created, day by difficult and wondrous day. Those days now stretch before you, already so full, still offering so much. Welcome to motherhood, Misfit Mom.

Epilogue

These babies aren't nearly as difficult as you feared, right? It's all just a simple matter of organization, of having and keeping a schedule, isn't it? Ha! Don't be so sure. Take a quick peek at your baby. Little Precious is getting so big—just starting to crawl! Throw a blanket and some toys on the floor and he or she actually remains happily occupied long enough for you to make a phone call, or whip up some dinner or—gasp—*read a magazine*! Imagine that! Not to mention all the sleep you've been getting since Baby gave up those crazy middle-of-the-night howling sessions. Feeling pretty good right now, aren't you? Things are finally under control at your house.

That's all going to change. Very soon.

Your beautiful baby will soon become a toddler. *Toddler* comes from the verb *toddle*, meaning to move with short, unsteady steps. It sounds adorably harmless and perfectly manageable. Guess again. Those steps may be short and unsteady, but your little one can cover a shocking amount of ground on those pudgy feet. Toddlers are famed for their *curiosity*, or desire to learn and know everything. You've heard what curiosity did to the cat—now it's going to wreak unholy havoc on your house and sanity. Toddlers, in addition to being energetic and curious, also lack what we call *common sense*. They don't understand the dangers inherent in fire, water, electricity, or heights. Toddler logic is absolutely simple. For example, if mommy puts toilet paper in the toilet, perhaps the TV remote belongs in there, too. And a toddler will not be reasoned with. Their concept of time is the perpetual *now*, meaning the promise of a future cookie or park outing will do absolutely nothing to persuade your pint-size dictator to behave properly in the present.

Based on careful observation, I would argue that the human toddler is, in fact, very similar to a new species of dinosaur, the skeletal remains of which were recently unearthed in Montana. Small, agile, carnivorous, and extremely swift, this new dinosaur, christened *nanotyrannosaurus*, is apparently related to the tyrannosaurus rex. Dubbed the *pygmy tyrant*, the nanotyrannosaurus roamed what are now the plains of the American west. Researchers got awfully excited over a pile of dirty bones, but we could have spared them a lot of unnecessary digging. There is a female pygmy tyrant living in captivity at our house right now. We call her *Toddlerasaurus Olivia Miss-Thingus*. Below are field notes culled from our study of this fascinating and tireless creature:

DAY ONE: The pygmy tyrant's preferred habitat is one of chaos. She carries books, dolls, toys, and empty cups from one area to another, leaving a trail of debris in her wake. Certain objects have acquired totemic status, including a scrap of plaid fabric aggressively protected by the pygmy tyrant. Attempts to remove said items result in angry bellowing and other threatening verbal displays. Primitive nesting behavior? Requires further analysis.

DAY TWO: Unable to establish creature's natural sleep/wake cycle. Varies wildly. Occasionally will not sleep at all, despite obvious fatigue. During these wakeful periods, the behavior of the pygmy tyrant is dangerously unpredictable. Enraged and sleepless pygmy tyrant flings wooden block at observer; surveillance temporarily halted due to injury.

DAY THREE: Despite the constant presence of grime on the creature's face, the question of grooming has been conclusively answered. The pygmy tyrant was witnessed wiping her own hands and face on a pre-moistened towelette. That the creature then tried to eat the towelette does not invalidate the finding, though it is worrisome.

DAY FOUR: Volatile temper to the contrary, the pygmy tyrant is a social creature and frequently seeks interaction with both adults and other juvenile tyrants. Fond of repetition, the tyrant frequently removes books from her nest area (see Day One), and uses them as crude tools to poke or whack nearby adults. Once adult attention is obtained, she squeals and roars until achieving her goal of having "Mr. Brown Can Moo! Can You?" read aloud for the umpteenth time.

DAY FIVE: The pygmy tyrant is surprisingly adept at manipulating electronics. Mesmerized by the dishwasher, she repeatedly yanked on the control knob, then removed and hid it. Moving to the oven, the tyrant worked tirelessly at its barely-out-of-reach knobs. Distracted from her task by a ringing phone, the creature hauled a cordless handset into her nest and dialed a random number in South Korea. Note: Scrutinize last month's mysteriously high phone bill.

DAY SIX: Don't let her diminutive stature fool you. The pygmy tyrant is fast. In one documented two-minute time period, the creature emptied a cupboard full of Tupperware, shoved her plastic alphabet letters under the refrigerator, dragged a bottle of Windex out of the laundry room, and swished her feet in the dog's water dish. An attempt to restrain the tyrant was met with belligerent, high-decibel wailing. Theory: Destructive behavior as a means of marking territory?

DAY SEVEN: Baffled by source of pygmy tyrant's boundless energy, as creature seems to consume nothing but Pepperidge Farm Goldfish, Cheerios, and milk. Experiments with hamburger have been successful, though all other foods are violently rejected. Vegetable matter in particular has been met with outright hostility, manifested in shrieking, head shaking, and the tossing of offending vegetable at researchers. Currently investigating the feasibility of rolling vegetables in dog hair and leaving them on the floor, since the pygmy tyrant is eager to put any item found in that condition into her mouth.

Field research was terminated after one week to allow participating observers to recover.

Scientists have concluded that it is remarkable for the pygmy tyrant, lacking size, strength, or superior tools, to be able to virtually control and dominate her surroundings. One promising theory suggests that the tyrant uses her considerable charm and beauty, along with effusive bursts of affection directed at her minders, to maintain her primacy in the environment. Though more data is called for, this study clearly indicates that only the very strongest, most adaptable organisms are able to coexist in harmony with the cunning, energetic, and mercurial pygmy tyrant. These organisms are easily identified by their haggard appearance, weary gait, and fierce devotion to the tyrant they serve. We call them *parents*.

Acknowledgments

Without my husband Mark's love, patience, and willingness to juggle every imaginable kind of craziness, I could not have written this book. Thank you for reading, correcting, printing, collating, debugging, solving all sorts of problems, and listening to the same things over and over again. I don't tell you enough how much I appreciate you.

I'm lucky to be surrounded by some of the finest people in broadcasting at Jefferson-Pilot Communications. Huge thanks to my radio partner and dear friend, Bob Lacey. He's like a brother, a confidant, and an extra husband all rolled into one. I wouldn't be here without him. My love and appreciation to Max Sweeten and Todd Haller, for their bottomless patience and steadiness. To Rick Jackson, for giving me his trust when just about anyone else in our business would have shown me the door. That support has meant the world to me. To Tony Garcia, who has treated this book as though it were his own, not to mention staking his entire career on *Bob & Sheri*. To Lisa Gergely, Sandra Mann, and all of my coworkers at WLNK—the best in radio.

And thanks to Tom Jackson, who first encouraged me to write and has been a faithful reader ever since.

To my agent, Marc Gerald, who combines all of the best aspects of fairy godmother, coach, and coconspirator: thanks for finding and believing in me. To my editor at St. Martin's, Elizabeth Beier, who possesses the enviable skill of making hard things seem easy, deadlines completely doable, and extra work a delightful opportunity. Thanks for making this so much fun.

For letting me scrutinize and endlessly question every aspect of their pregnancies, births, and child-rearing techniques—without once losing their sense of humor—I owe a tremendous debt to my favorite Misfit Moms: Marsha Ferebee, Renee Gramaglia, Nancy Lynch, and Anne Oberlander. For being a good sport and giving me her unconditional love and support even while I critiqued some of her maternal methods, thanks to my mom, Frances Jorgensen. Finally, for teaching me about courage, grace, strength, and how life *really* works, I thank the countless women who have called, written, and listened to our radio show for the past decade. Because of you, I feel like I have sisters everywhere.

Index